RawnMade

A Lifetime of Magical Tools

Rawn Clark

RawnMade
A Lifetime of Magical Tools
By Rawn Clark

CONTENTS

INTRODUCTION

What exactly is a "magical tool"?

The most rudimentary definition of a magical tool is: any thing that functions as an aide to the performance of a magical act. This can be anything from the small stone I carry in my pocket; to a sword or wand used in ritual; to a statue or image of a deity used in worship. *Any* thing that aides your awareness or abilities in pursuit of magic (whatever that may mean to you).

Within this definition, I find four categories or classes:

1) A tool that is a "found" special thing or memento.
2) A tool that has no power of its own and all power comes from the user.
3) A tool that has its own power but requires a user to activate.
4) A tool that has its own power and does not need a user to activate.

The first class of tool has no intrinsic power except that it reminds you of a moment, an experience, a place or feeling. These are "found" items or items that seem given by the universe. An example is the stone I carry in my pocket.

The second class in usually made but can also be a "found" object. An example is a traditional wand: its power comes solely from the user and energy is passed *through* it. This sort can accumulate power over time but any such charge is generated strictly by its repeated use. Another example would be a statue of a favored Deity which helps to focus the magician's mind or devotion.

The third class of tool is like an automobile: it has the potential for great power but is of no use without a driver. An example of this sort would be my *Gate Maker*, which has a charge but only becomes useful and effective when a user projects their awareness into it.

The fourth class is the most unusual since it is *always* magically active and has the ability to affect anyone who encounters it. Examples of this kind might be a "holy relic" that heals instantly, or my own *Radiator* which continuously radiates the Kethric Brilliance.

Magical tools can be made things or natural things: supremely simple or grandly complex and all be just as beneficial to the user. In the case of the first two classes of tools (those that simply aid and have no inherent power of their own) it matters little what materials the tool is made from or its shape, size, color, etc., **beyond what has the most appropriate meaning to the user.**

In other words, the power exerted by the tool comes *solely* from the user and relies on the mental and astral connection the *user* has with the symbolism inherent in the tool's form. If the sword means absolutely nothing to the one who lifts it, it will be just a heavy weight; but in the hands of one who understands its meaning, it will be a powerful way to wield their authority. My pocket stone may be just an ugly rock to another, but to me it is a thing of great beauty and significance! Although it has a life of its own that speaks to me, it is still *me* who has invested this power in the stone.

In the third and fourth class of tools that I mentioned above – the ones that possess an inherent power of their own – the make-up of the tool is almost always of great importance. In fact I can't think of a case where this is not so. There is, of course, the symbolic importance that must be in tune with the user (if there is a user); it must *look* appropriate. Then there is the matter of employing the right materials for use with the specific energies to be generated, manipulated, channeled, etc. For example, with some energies I will want my tool to be made out of copper; with others, out of wood; and still others, out of crystal or ice. In general, *the energy determines the material and the symbolic meaning determines the form.*

How is a magical tool made?

It takes no special skill or ability to make a magical tool! Sometimes, the most powerful tool can be something you simply "find" along a river or on a walk in the woods or down the street even. You see, there are no rules here; no requirements that a tool be made out of this or that material, or in this or that way, etc. A tool must only fit its intended purpose so however you can achieve that goal, no matter what the material or shape it takes, it is the *right* way.

There are really only two requirements in making a tool: *intention* and *attention*. To make a magical tool you must concentrate with your whole awareness on what you are doing and why you are doing it, throughout the *whole* assembly process. You must be filled with intention about the tool and focused only on your goal, because it is these two factors that render it *magical*. Done correctly, the crudest, ugliest looking thing can become a very powerful and useful tool!

Of course the substance you make a tool out of will in great part determine what the tool is capable of, especially when it comes to the storage and movement of energy. Some substances are best for projecting energy, some for storing and accumulating energy, some for amplifying energy and some for condensing energy. Some are capable of several of these abilities simultaneously depending upon the intent and how they are juxtaposed or combined.

In my own work making tools, I've found the following materials ideal for the five basic functions of an energy tool (a tool that in some way moves or stores or radiates energy):

* Flow or transmit
  A small tree branch (best harvested on the full moon).
  Any dried plant stem or branch that has a directional fiber.
  Gold, silver and copper wire.
  Copper tubing.
  Clear quartz crystal points (either single- or double-terminated).

* Projection
  A small tree branch or dried plant stem.
  Clear quartz crystal points. [*The* best, especially if double-terminated and unpolished!]
  Most other crystalline minerals that form points.
  Copper tubing.
  A gold, iron or copper rod (or pretty much anything with a rod shape if you're really good at projecting energy).

* Radiation without transmutation
  Clear quartz crystal spheres ("water clear"). [By far *the* best!]

* Storage, capture or accumulation
  Clear quartz spheres and points (storage, capture or accumulation).
  Gold and silver (storage or accumulation).
  Quartz spheres and points of any color, clear or opaque (storage).
  Certain river rocks (storage or capture).
  Obsidian in any form (capture).
  Raw turquoise (capture).
  Lead and hematite (capture)

* Transmutation
  Clear quartz of any form (but only with "instruction").
  Colored quartz (when energy is passed through it).
  Fluorites or tourmalines (when energy is passed through it).

In reality, a trained magician is able (or should be) to use **anything** as a tool, but these substances will naturally facilitate the magician's work and are therefore good choices when tool making.

Care must also be taken in choosing things to use *with* these substances in the construction of a tool. Wood for example, has a grain which will channel energy to some extent: but do you want that in your tool or do you want something that is energetically neutral like clay or cardboard (which is the primary reason I use it)? Glass will act as an insulator and that can either be advantageous or detrimental, etc. You can create all the crystal and wire circuitry you want but if you use the wrong material to support it, you can end up shorting it out! So care must be taken and you should investigate the energetic properties of the supplementary materials you choose.

So if you want to make a magical tool, stop and really think about it. Ask yourself what you want it to do and why. Figure out what would be the best material(s) to use to accomplish what you want from the tool. Can you procure or find them or do you need to adapt and improvise? Once you figure out the what, why and how bits, make a plan and do it. It's always good to have a plan even if it evolves as you go! Ha!

How do I use a magical tool?

This of course depends upon the tool itself; there is no one way. The main constant is the attitude one should adopt beforehand. At the very least, there must be seriousness and focus; your attention must be "in the now" and fully on what you are doing. A trained magician should adopt a tri-polar (physio-astra-mental) awareness (at least) when working with a tool as this is the way to get the most out of a tool's use.

Some tools will come with instructions and as you will find out in what follows, sometimes those can be very elaborate and detailed. It can also just be visually obvious as with a wand or sword. Or, when in doubt, you can just ask the tool's maker or the tool itself!

So now, I will move on to describing and showing you examples of all four of these classes of magical tool from my own opus . . .

FIRST CLASS

Our first class of magical tool (those special "found" objects) has been a part of my life since the beginning and is at the root of my earliest memories. It seems that I've always had a special stone in my pocket or a collection of special feathers; and then later, a collection of really cool sticks and small branches. Each of these "found" objects (but they all feel like gifts from the Universe when first received) served as inspirations that reminded me of the miracle of the natural world – a thing which has *always* captivated my imagination. Through them I would connect with the spirit of a place, time or event that felt special at the time. Mostly, they would stay with me for only a short time, a few months at the most, except for one: the rock that has resided in my pocket by itself (so that nothing scratches its surface) for about 30 years now. . .

The Pocket Stone

For several years back in the 1990's, I lived in the small (really small) little town of Laytonville, in northern California. I was situated just north of town, on a dirt road (or rather, a dust or a mud road depending on the time of year) called Woodman Creek Road. The town's whole economy seemed to be based on the (illegal at the time) cultivation of some of the world's best cannabis and so most of my neighbors and friend were "pot growers". A wonderful class of people by the way!

At that time, my best friend, Garrett, and I were working as "trimmers" for the pot harvest – we called ourselves "Crew Cut" and were quite famous in our own way for our speed, accuracy and entertainment value! Ah, but this time is filled with so many happy memories . . .

At any rate, Woodman Creek Road winds its way east from the Hwy101 to the South Fork of the Eel River and ends at a large, natural bed-rock beach where the water was only neck-deep all the way across and not too swift so as to knock you over. The perfect spot at which to enjoy the River with no sign of human imprint! Just you and the rattlesnakes and bears and cougars and deer and birds and bazillions of insects. And . . . an infinity of rocks. Heaven!

In the late summer or early autumn of 1993 or 1994, all the pot growers out Woodman way had a big overnight Full Moon party for all the neighbors and workers and Garrett and I were invited. There were probably about 30-40 humans all told, every one of which brought something to eat, drink or smoke. *ALL* of the best Woodman grown weed and hash, fresh abalone just caught off the pacific coast, local bear and deer meat, and a bounty of fresh local garden produce of every kind! It was a feast for the ages and just an amazing time of friendship and sharing.

After spending endless hours in and out of the River and watching all the wildlife pass by (a rattlesnake by the big boulder; a deer being stalked by a cougar; several hawks and an eagle overhead; dragonflies galore) I decided to retire to the beach rocks for a close-up look around. This, of course, is one of my lifelong most favoritest past-times – looking at rocks! And here was about a half-mile of rock beach for me to get lost in before the sun got too low. As I said before: heaven!

You know that feeling you get when you just *know* something special is about to happen or that you will find a jewel in the dirt at your feet? Well, that's the feeling I had from the moment I began looking at the rocks. I learned a long time before that you can't look _for_ those really special rocks . . . they're gifts that are _given_ and you have to get into that head space of just appreciating everything you see for its own uniqueness. Just look for looking's sake, not for wanting's sake and the River will present whatever it has to present. And after just a few steps along the water's edge, the River responded . . . with **THE** stone that I *needed* to have, at just the right moment in my life.

A flash of root-beer orange between shadows caused by the ripples of water and the immediate recognition of translucence made me stop in my tracks and bend further over to snatch it out of the River's grasp. Eureka! Halleluiah! Praise the Goddess! Holy Shit! WOW! The most beatifullest rock *ever*!

Now don't get me wrong, I like _all_ rocks; they all have something of interest to say to me and always have since I popped out of my mother's womb! But my most favorite are rocks that play with the sunlight or moonlight in some way. Rocks that reflect are nice but those that take the light into their bodies attract me the most. They are special above all others and different in their ways: they become at one _with_ the light and are transformed; their song changes and brightens as it reveals details of their inner beauty. This rock did all that and more . . .

It was gloriously smooth and warm to the touch and fit perfectly in the palm of my hand. Then I held it up to the sun and it glowed the most sublime, bright yet rich, golden tone of orangey honey-brown. It radiated a tangible warmth, a sort of cozy yumminess. And in its center I began to see a cosmos of little dark lines take shape and finally resolve into a peculiarly evocative shape.

I was very moved by this stone. I could feel that it had something very important and powerful to tell me. I sat down right there, at water's edge and thanked the River for its wonderful gift and just sat with it, in my hand, trying to hear its words. But I could tell that this was neither the place nor time for the fullness of _that_ conversation.

Any time you encounter a "found" tool that comes with that feeling of it being more important somehow, you can bet that is has either been touched with intention by another human, or it has been chosen by and astra-mental "nature spirit" or such, to teach you something. It's **always** worthwhile to give it a listen!

SECOND CLASS

SECTION TWO

The Wand

An example of the second class of tool (a tool that has no power of its own and all power comes from the user) is a wand I made in the year or so before I encountered my pocket rock. It is a combination of "found" and made, but to tell that story, I must tell you the broader story of Rishallah and Ishiwah . . .

Right before moving of Laytonville, I lived northeast of the smallish town of Willits, California. I lived atop a hill, overlooking a valley surrounded by other small hills and some actual mountains in the distance to the east. I had walking access to about 300 acres of formerly logged forest that was now a mixed wood of oaks, second or third growth redwood, fir and madrone. It was beautiful and just my kind of place to roam for endless hours getting to know all the rocks and insects and little critters. I was in heaven!

While roaming the land one day, I came across a fairly sizable (6' diameter?), plain looking and very flat rock which brought me to a stop. It felt important so I sat with it a while. I was quickly moved to sit on the stone, in its center and when I did, I felt Her presence . . . The presence felt sort of melancholy, yet happy and relieved at the same time. I reached out astra-mentally and She resolved into what appeared to be a native woman about my own age, wearing deer skin garments with lots of stone ornaments and feathers about Her head.

As you've noticed, I've been capitalizing 'Her' and 'She' because there was this immediate sense of immense significance about Her, as if She were a goddess of some sort or, at the least, one who has been worshipped by many. Her image seemed to switch back and forth between a youngish woman and a very, very old Grandmother; both equally appealing and equally ordinary at the same time. *Very* human and relatable.

Her name is Rishallah. She was worshipped here and cared for the people of this land, a long, long, long time ago – perhaps thousands of years ago – for a long, long time, but all her people had died a long, long time ago, hence Her happiness that I had noticed Her and stopped to tarry a while. It had been so, so long since anyone had even thought of Her, let alone spoken Her name . . . Yet She still watched over the land and all who passed Her way; ever vigilant and ever protective.

After a time, She spoke of Her lover, Ishiwah, who She hadn't seen in an awfully long time. She was almost shy with remorse and longing for Him. It was sweet . . . It turned out that the only way they could meet was through a ritual performed by Her worshippers and there hadn't been any for such a long time! She told me great stories of what He did for the people and the land and about how much She missed Him.

So I asked Her if I could help Her or Them in some way . . . Our plan then was for me to try to replicate the original ritual that Her worshippers used to perform to bring Them together! Hopefully we would be able to Unify them permanently since I wouldn't be around for ever. Ha! So, a Grand Ritual of Unification it was to be then!

First I would need to locate and craft a Wand for Rishallah and Ishiwah. Within a couple of days, I found the perfect stick to make the Wand out of: a little over a foot long, as thick as my middle finger and looking exactly like an uncoiled snake, head and tapered tail to boot! So I brought it home and got to work.

I did a little subtle carving on the head end to accentuate its snake features and painted the whole half of the stick in metallic gold. I then inserted small faceted pieces of emerald glass in its eyes and put a small double-terminated clear quartz crystal in its open mouth.

I then painted the tail end with metallic silver paint and braided some red and black leather in the middle: a black knot at each end to define the head and tail, and a red and black swirl in between. [I only have two poor quality cropped photos of the Wand sitting on a past altar to show you unfortunately. One of the whole of it, but behind other altar furnishings and one clearer of its tail end.]

When I was finished, I took the Wand back to the flat stone and conferred with Rishallah. She really, really liked it! High praise coming from a Goddess and all! Ha! At any rate, my ego all boosted everything, She began instructing me in the Wand's dedication ceremony and its manner of use. The ceremony was a simple dedication ritual and all I needed were some herbs from the local area for incense. Its use though, was a bit more involved.

When held with the head upright, it represented and evoked Rishallah's desire for Her Lover. When held with the *tail* upward, it represented and evoked Ishiwah's desire for His lover. In the Unification Ritual, the Wand is to be held outward at shoulder height and flipped back and forth between head-up and head-down, head-up, head-down, over and over and over until a certain ecstatic state of trance is achieved, At that point Rishallah and Ishiwah unite and the Wand is held horizontally. . .

It turned out to be the old romance between Moon and Sun! In order for them to unite *through Rishallah and Ishiwah* a ritual had to be performed at every full and every new moon. At the full moon, Rishallah and Ishiwah see each other clearly from afar and their desire for one another is great, palpable in the air, everyone feels it, even the plants and animals. On the night of the fullest moon, when their desire has reached its peak the Ritual of Unification is performed and they are United.

Ordinarily – in the distant past – Ishiwah would carry Rishallah away to return Her at the new moon to the people and the Ritual of Return would be performed. Between the new and full moons, Rishallah would reside on Her own with the people. But we were going for something more this time: there was to be no Ritual of Return for Rishallah on this occasion.

All that was needed was Ishiwah's agreement and help, which of course was not an issue and he eagerly consented, excited by the possibilities. With Ishiwah's help, the three of us together were able to sever Rishallah's ties to the land and its creatures, and set her finally free to join Her Ishiwah forever more . . .

And that was that: goodbye Rishallah and Ishiwah. I continued to feel an echo of Her every time I walked the land but I think that was just the land remembering; either that or She looks in on it every new moon when She's close at hand . . .

At that point in my magical journey (mid 30's) I felt a lack of worship in my practice (the fact that this need coincided with meeting Rishallah is, well, no coincidence) so to meet that need, I joined a Wiccan coven to be educated in Goddess worship. This inspired me to make another tool: a Goddess statue inspired by Rishallah (although it looks nothing like Her) . . .

The Goddess Statue

From my late teens through my mid-20's, my artistic medium of choice was clay, but I drifted away from it eventually for several reasons mostly having to do with the lack of access to a kiln. However, I could think of no better medium (for me) than clay for this statue so I bought some low-fire red clay and set to work with the expectation / hope that I would find someone to fire it for me later.

I finished it in early summer but by mid-autumn I still hadn't found anybody local to fire it. Fortunately (as it turned out), it had been a hot dry summer and the statue had dried so thoroughly that it was basically rock hard, so I decided to work with what I had and finish the piece as it was. The only weak part of the dried clay structure was the hair I had given Her: long, ropey dreads, so I removed those and began decorating! Here's what I did to Her –

I painted Her body with a rather bizarre mixture, the basis of which I would use for the next 30 years and still use today: 1 part acrylic paint (a very, very dark purple almost black), 3 parts *Elmer's Glue-All* (a popular brand of PVA glue), and an eclectic mixture of quartz crystal dust and roughly ground mother-of-pearl (to sparkle in the candlelight). The water I used to thin this concoction was a prepared Liquid Fluid Condenser made with gold and chamomile (per F. Bardon).

Next, I painted Her face with the same sort of mixture only in a dull, earthy red with blue, black and green details.

Then I painted Her hands and feet in colors that would depict the Fluidic and Elemental, right-left equilibrium (sort of): Right hand = red/Fire; Right foot = orange/Air; Left hand = blue/Water; Left foot = green/Earth.

Last in painting sequence, were the spirals: light purple on Her breast and pale blue on Her belly.

Then came the most fun part of all: decorating Rishallah with all Her splendid finery! First came the disks She holds in each hand – whose making ignited a 30 year long love affair with, of all things, cardboard! Ha!

These disks were *very* first things **ever** that I made out of cardboard! As most of you know, cardboard has become my medium of choice for constructing all my forms, but at that moment it was matter of necessity – it was all I had on hand to work with! [Later it became "the only thing I could afford": a.k.a., FREE, but that's another story for another time.]

So, two pieces of cardboard glued together; painted; gold wire (right hand / electric) and silver wire (left hand / magnetic) around the edge; with strings of beads hanging at intervals. The right hand disk represented the Electric Fluid and the left, the Magnetic Fluid. [Sorry, no close-up of the left.]

Then She got Her necklace, which is a bronze serpent head with a red carnelian set in its mouth on a gold chain, then small emerald stud earrings (that can't be seen under her hair), and Her hair of local Spanish moss. To top it all off, She got an elaborate headdress:

First a layer of the downy breast feathers from an owl I "found" dead on the roadside not too long before; then a bit more of the moss; topped by a rope of red beads spiraled around to form a seat for the dried Echinacea flower finial. At the back of Her headdress is the same owl's entire tail. Draped over the tail were strings of real gold beads on gold tread.

She was, of course, hollow, with a large lower vaginal opening and openings at Her mouth, ears and several holes in Her scalp. This was designed so that a cone of incense burning in front of Her vaginal opening would, after filling the whole interior with smoke, slowly trail smoke out of Her mouth and ears and top of Her head!

21

She graced my main working altar as the center piece for all the years I spent in coven. As a magical tool of the first class, She had no inherent power of Her own yet served to focus my practice of Goddess worship perfectly. I learned so much with Her over time: just what I needed to learn apparently!

The Walking Stick / Staff

The next example of the second class of tools I have to present from my past is the walking stick or short Staff I made around the same time.

It was made out of a branch from a Madrone tree, cut for me specially on request by my dear friend, Don, on his property north of Laytonville. It was a little over three foot long and I ended up modifying it only slightly. I put a thimble on the bottom to protect it from wear and then applied some *ritually* braided red and black leather as a knob on the top and a hand-hold about mid-way down.

I don't know if you've ever braided leather but it's not that easy! It took me hours and hours to do the top knot! A **lot** of intention and magical spellwork went into it (and probably a few swear words if I remember correctly)!

After a consecration ritual it became a very useful tool over the years. It provided grounding and stability when used as a Walking Stick, and functioned as a good channel for energies of various sorts when used as a Staff. Every bit of its power and significance came from my astra-mental connection with it and flowed from my hand into and through it.

The Magic Mirror Box / The Communicator

The next example follows pretty closely on the heels of the Goddess statue and is the **very** first cardboard *construction* I ever made. It fits in this category of the second class of tool because to merely houses and amplifies an already existing tool that I had been using for a while already. That this is my first go at constructing a tool out of cardboard amazes me to this day. It stands out as one of *the* most complex and functional constructions I've ever achieved. Right up there near the top of the list!

This is my Magic Mirror Box or The Communicator as it later became known. It began life in the summer of 1999 but was converted to use by the old TMO

Working Group (a group I started in 2005 to explore the possibilities of working TMO in a group context) in 2006. Here follows the official TMO-WG "user's manual" for the Communicator that tells everything to know about it.

THE COMMUNICATOR

A User Manual
By Rawn Clark
July 2006

INTRODUCTION:

Originally constructed in June of 1999 as a permanent home for my personal magic mirror, The Communicator was the very first tool used by the TMO-WG. Initially, it was known simply as the Magic Mirror and was employed to create a beacon of Light which drew the Working Group members together in our meeting place during each of our group rituals. Because of the six-sided nature of the Magic Mirror, each Working Group was limited to six members and each member was assigned to a colored side of the Magic Mirror during group work. However, as the TMO-WG began to grow in number, the limitation of six members per WG imposed by the use of the Magic Mirror became problematic and use of the Magic Mirror as our primary tool became less than optimal. Eventually, we abandoned the six-member limitation and incorporated the use of other tools.

With the advent of The Integrator, The Unifier and The Consecrator, it became apparent that our Magic Mirror needed to evolve into broader use and so it became known as The Communicator. As The Communicator, it is assigned to the East Quarter under the aegis of Raphael, Guardian of the Air Element. After its first few initial uses in this context, it became obvious that it required a refurbishing to truly evolve from being our former Magic Mirror to becoming fully functional as The Communicator, so in late June of 2006, it received a thorough overhaul.

This refurbishing entailed a new coat of paint to all surfaces, an adjustment to the contents of all 12 drawers, the addition of a solid-Fluid condenser surrounding the mirror itself, and the creation of a Silk Shroud.

As with the other tools dedicated to TMO-WG use, The Communicator now belongs to the TMO-WG Unity as a whole and will be passed on to the care of a responsible member of the Unity upon my death.

STRUCTURE:

The basic structure of The Communicator is formed out of cardboard and synthetic-felt (used for the hinges of the six leaves that form the lid, to line each drawer and to protect the bottom). All surfaces have been painted with a mixture of Elmer's Glue-All® and acrylic paint.

Essentially, The Communicator is a traditional magic mirror composed of several Fluid condensers supporting a concave Obsidian mirror-disk. There are three levels to The Communicator.

Level One: The Six Bottom Drawers

Each of these drawers is filled with select Obsidian pieces that I have collected over the years. Each piece of Obsidian is an ancient stone tool crafted by the aboriginal residents of Northern California. Some are small knife blades, others are arrow points and still others are small scrapers. [The one exception is a small Flint knife blade in the green drawer.]

These items serve as grounding solid-Fluid condensers and as hand-crafted stone tools, they infer an additional degree of functional intention to the grounding of The Communicator.

Level Two: The Six Top Drawers

These drawers are filled with a mixture of aboriginal stone tools (small knife blades, arrow points and scrapers) made of local (Northern California) multi-colored Flint, along with one double-terminated clear Quartz crystal (from Arkansas) per drawer. In addition, there is a local blue-green Jade healing stone (Blue drawer), a small "spirit stone" figurine (Orange drawer), and a (modern) gold pentagram (Yellow drawer). Each stone piece was selected from my personal collection of found items discovered during my years of walking Northern California creek beds and country side.

These items serve as more expansive solid-Fluid condensers. Each of the hand-crafted stone tools infers both functional intention as well as the desire of the maker to create something of beauty.

Level Three: The Lidded Mirror Cabinet

Surrounding the Mirror itself are 13 rounded stones of graduated sizes. These were all found in the same creek bed and were tumbled perfectly round by water. These serve as a solid-condenser of the Magnetic Fluid.

Atop these stones surrounding the Mirror is a circlet of braided Gold, Silver and Copper wires. This serves as a solid Universal Fluid condenser.

Directly beneath the concave Obsidian Mirror is a circular Tarot card (the 10 of Pentacles from the Daughters of the Moon Tarot) which has been saturated with a liquid Universal Fluid condenser. And set atop the Obsidian Mirror is a string of very fine natural Pearls which serve as a solid condenser of the Magnetic Fluid.

The Communicator is hexagonal to represent the conjunction of Macro- and Microcosm. Each side is given a planetary color (Purple=Moon, Blue=Jupiter, Green=Venus, Yellow=Sun, Orange=Mercury, and Red=Mars) while the topmost point of the lid is given the color of Saturn (Violet) set in a golden hexagon.

The lid opens like the petals of a lotus flower –

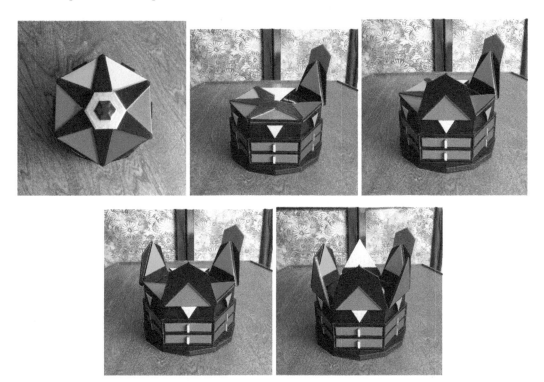

To reveal the mirror within –

And, of course, The Communicator has its own tailored Silk Shroud –

USING THE COMMUNICATOR:

Function #1: Communication

The primary function of The Communicator is that of projecting and receiving communications between the members of the TMO-WG. Ordinarily, this ability relies upon mastery of the Akasha but because of the structure of The Communicator, the Kethric Brilliance is used instead of the Akasha. The Kethric Brilliance is the source of the Akasha and as such, contains all of the properties of Akasha -- specifically its ability to serve as a connecting medium between all things, regardless of spatial and/or temporal distance.

To prepare The Communicator for use, its Silk Shroud is removed and then the six leaves or petals of its lid are opened to reveal the mirror disk. Next, all participants must accumulate the Kethric Brilliance and project it as a cloud which surrounds The Communicator. The Communicator will then automatically draw the Kethric Brilliance inward through the contents of its 12 drawers and after a few moments, the Kethric Brilliance arises to cover the surface of the mirror disk like a coating of dew. The accumulation and projection of Kethric Brilliance is repeated until the mirror surface becomes completely saturated with the Brilliance.

Those participants who wish to **receive** a message (i.e., an image, sound, idea, etc.) must accumulate the Kethric Brilliance individually and condense the Brilliance within the organ of perception they wish to use. For example, if the reception of a visual communication is desired, then the Brilliance is concentrated within the eyes; or within the ears for an audible communication; etc. If reception of a multi-sensorial communication is desired, then each of the relevant sensory organs must be filled with the Brilliance (e.g., the eyes *and* ears for an audio-visual communication). If the communication is to be in the form of an idea, then the Kethric Brilliance must be condensed within the mental body or awareness of the receiver, and if an emotion is to be received, the Brilliance is condensed within the astral body as a whole. Alternately, the Kethric Brilliance may be accumulated within the *entire* physio-astra-mental body, thus enabling the reception of any sort of communication.

Once the organ/body is filled with the Kethric Brilliance, the receiver must meditate upon the fact that the Kethric Brilliance serves to connect receiver and sender, regardless of spatial and/or temporal distance, *through* The Communicator's mirror disk. Once the receiver is convinced of the connecting power of the Kethric Brilliance, attention is focused upon the surface of the mirror disk and the receiver passively awaits the incoming message.

Meanwhile, the **sender** spends several moments meditating upon the fact that the Kethric Brilliance which saturates the surface of the mirror disk connects sender and receiver, regardless of spatial and/or temporal distance. The sender must feel as if they are standing right next to the receiver(s).

Once the sender is convinced of this fact, they must intensively focus their chosen message upon the surface of the mirror disk to such a degree that it becomes perceptible to the receiver. If an image is being sent, then the sender must see the image floating upon the mirror surface concretely. If a sound is being sent, then the sender must concretely hear the sound and cause it to pass *through* the mirror so that the receiver hears it. Similarly, if an idea or emotion is sent, the sender must concretely experience it for themselves and then send it *through* to mirror disk to the receiver. The sender must always imagine concretely that the receiver is in fact, perceiving their sent message.

If the communication is to be reciprocated (i.e., if the sender wishes to then *receive* a message from the former receiver), then the roles must be reversed. This means that the former sender must accumulate the Kethric Brilliance in whatever organ (or combination of organs) of perception is most appropriate and meditate upon the fact that the While Brilliance serves to connect them with the sender, regardless of the spatial and/or temporal distance separating them. Once convinced of this fact, the now-receiver focuses attention upon the surface of the mirror disk and passively awaits the incoming message.

Meanwhile, the former-receiver meditates upon the fact that the Kethric Brilliance which saturates the surface of the mirror disk connects them with the now-receiver. And once convinced of this fact, the now-sender concretely projects their message upon/through the mirror.

If a back-and-forth conversation is desired, *both* parties must accumulate the Kethric Brilliance into the necessary organ(s) of perception (only once) and then alternate between active projection and passive reception.

When the communication session is finished, all messages are dissipated (i.e., images dissolved, ideas terminated, etc.) from the surface of the mirror and the connection between sender and receiver is consciously severed. The petals of The Communicator's lid are then closed to hide the mirror and it is re-covered with its Silk Shroud.

There is no need to cleanse The Communicator of the accumulated Kethric Brilliance when the session is finished. In fact, it is best if the accumulation is intentionally left within The Communicator so that it builds over time. This will make The Communicator more and more powerful with each successive use.

Function #2: Establishing a Doorway

The mirror surface of The Communicator may easily be used to create a doorway between the participants and any other realm, planetary zone, entity and/or person. Once the doorway is established, the participants may either project their own awareness through the doorway or they may project an influence through the doorway so that it affects whom- or whatever lies on the other side. For example, a doorway may be established between the participants and a healing subject and a healing influence may then be projected through the doorway so that it directly affects the healing subject.

To begin, The Communicator is un-Shrouded and the petals of the lid are opened to reveal the mirror disk. The participants then accumulate the Kethric Brilliance and condense it as a cloud which surrounds The Communicator. The accumulation and projection is repeated until the surface of the mirror is sufficiently saturated with the Kethric Brilliance.

Then all participants must focus upon the fact that the Brilliance connects them with the person or realm they wish, regardless of any spatial or temporal distance between them. If the doorway is to connect with a person, then that person must be concretely visualized within the mirror surface and the participants must feel as if they are standing right next to the person. Similarly, if connection with a planetary zone or realm is desired, then the qualities of the zone or realm must be concretely manifest upon the mirror's surface through an intensive act of will and imagination.

Once the doorway is concretely established it may be used. An influence (e.g., a healing energy) may be projected through the doorway by an intensive act of will and imagination. Or, the awareness' of the participants may be projected through the doorway by imagination and will.

When the session is complete, the doorway is dissolved by will and imagination, and the connection is severed. The petals of the lid are closed and The Communicator is re-Shrouded.

Again, it is not necessary to cleanse The Communicator of the accumulated Kethric Brilliance.

Function #3: Observation From Afar

The Communicator may be used as a sort of telescope through which participants may passively observe other places and times. This is similar to creating a doorway except that it is *one-way only*, instead of a passage through which influences and/or awareness' may pass.

To begin, The Communicator is un-Shrouded and the petals of the lid are opened to reveal the mirror disk. The participants then accumulate the Kethric Brilliance and condense it as a cloud which surrounds The Communicator. The accumulation and projection is repeated until the surface of the mirror is sufficiently saturated with the Kethric Brilliance.

Next, the participants accumulate the Kethric Brilliance individually and concentrate it within the relevant organs of perception that they wish to use in their observation. For example, the eyes and ears, or the entire astra-mental body, depending upon how comprehensive the observation is to be.

Once the mirror's surface and the relevant sensory organs of the participants are sufficiently loaded with the Kethric Brilliance, all participants focus intensively upon the fact that the Kethric Brilliance connects them with the object of their observation. The object is then visualized upon the mirror's surface so concretely that the participants are able to truly perceive it. Once accomplished, the participants passively observe the desired object (i.e., the chosen person, place, time, etc.).

When the session is complete, the visualization of the object is dissolved by will and imagination, and the connection is severed. The petals of the lid are closed and The Communicator is re-Shrouded. All participants then rid their sensory organs of the accumulated Kethric Brilliance.

Again, it is not necessary to cleanse The Communicator of the accumulated Kethric Brilliance.

Function #4: Akashic Shielding

It is sometimes advantageous to encapsulate a person, thing, action and/or temporal duration within a "bubble" of the Akasha. This effectively removes the encapsulated subject from the effects of time-space and renders it astra-mentally "invisible" to external influences within the sequential realm. The only influences that can affect an encapsulated thing are the forces of its own personal karma, and any influences projected by the person who performed the encapsulation (and/or those given permission by the person who performed the encapsulation).

For example, all of the tools I have created for use by the TMO-WG Unity have each been individually encapsulated in an Akashic shield of this sort. This protects them from all influences except those approved by the members of the TMO-WG Unity and renders them astra-mentally invisible to all except us.

Similarly, each of the original meditation rituals of the 8 Temples Meditation Project were encapsulated within Akashic "bubbles". This preserves the purity of those specific temporal durations so that all who visit them may participate in the original working. Furthermore, their Akashic "bubbles" make them invisible and impervious to all external astra-mental influences. These rituals, thus encapsulated, can be accessed *only* by following the inherent sequence of visualizations described in the 8 Temples – this is what grants a person my *permission* to enter.

An Akashic shield can also be very beneficial when a person is the target of unwanted external negative influences that are not strictly karmic in origin. This can even temporarily alleviate some negative karmic influences thus providing the individual an opportunity to address the karmic issue through less negative means. However, if the karmic issue is not addressed, then not even an Akashic shield can prevent the negative consequences from being realized. Such a shield renders the individual completely invisible to non-karmic astra-mental influences, which causes said influences to exhaust themselves having found no "target" upon which to unleash their energy. [Once the energy has exhausted itself and the person is "safe", the Akashic shield should be dissolved.]

For the developing magician, an Akashic shield is also quite useful as a component of a triple (i.e., physical, astral and mental combined) shield, but it must be programmed to exclude only non-karmic negative influences of an especially

32

pernicious nature. There is a certain type or "species" of pernicious astra-mental energy that "likes" to test developing magicians and feed from the negative reactions (especially fear and its child, anger) which it can generate. One way to "pass" these tests during the early stages of magical development is to create one's own Akashic shield. This is because such astra-mental entities can only "see" those who contain within themselves something that is: a) worthy of testing; and, b) susceptible to disruption. In other words, they cannot "see" those who have attained the astral Equilibrium of the Elements, so until one has attained this Equilibrium, it is beneficial to use an Akashic shield to create the functional illusion of insusceptibility to disruption.

The procedure for creating an Akashic "bubble" is as follows –

To begin, The Communicator is un-Shrouded and the petals of the lid are opened to reveal the mirror disk. The participants then accumulate the Kethric Brilliance and condense it as a cloud which surrounds The Communicator. The accumulation and projection is repeated until the surface of the mirror is completely saturated with the Kethric Brilliance.

Next, the participants again accumulate the Kethric Brilliance but this time, instead of projecting it at The Communicator, it is projected as a radiant sphere, hovering directly above the mirror's surface. Projection is repeated/continued until the sphere is approximately 6" (15cm) in circumference and intensely radiant.

At this point, all participants must, through intensive will and imagination, transform this sphere of Kethric Brilliance into pure Akasha by imparting all of the qualities of the Akasha to the Kethric Brilliance. The specific qualities are a very dark Violet color, a sense of timelessness and spacelessness (i.e., immateriality), and invisibility (i.e., light passes completely *through* it without distortion). Then the Akasha is impregnated with the relevant instructions regarding its purpose, duration, etc.

When the transformation and impregnation is complete, the participants will either visualize the subject as being within the Akashic "bubble" or they will expand the "bubble" so that it surrounds the subject. If a person or object is being encapsulated, then it is best to visualize the subject within the sphere. But if a specific temporal duration or an action (e.g., a ritual) is to be encapsulated, then it is best to expand the "bubble" so that it completely encompasses the time span / action from beginning to end.

When the session is complete, the visualizations of the Akashic sphere and the subject are dissolved and the connection is severed. The petals of the lid are closed and The Communicator is re-Shrouded. Again, it is not necessary to cleanse The Communicator of the accumulated Kethric Brilliance.

So The Communicator was a tool for a tool. Before it was made, my Magic Mirror stood alone and the only Fluid Condensers used were liquid ones applied to the surface of the Mirror during use. Plus it had a nice piece of silk to cover it and that was all. So the tool of the box that I made enabled me to incorporate a broad range of Fluid Condensers more to my liking (chipped stone, crystals, metal, etc.) and turned my lowly Magic Mirror into a much more versatile tool that I ended up using more often thereafter. Then, when it came time for it to become one of the primary tools of the TMO-WG, it was a fairly simple matter of reorganizing the contents of its drawers, re-consecrating it, and voila, it became The Communicator.

The Purple Swan Rattle

My next example of a second class tool is a gift I made for some of my first "hermetic visitors" back in the early 2000's. [In 2002 I started actively accepting visitors to talk about hermetics and Franz Bardon's work, kabbalah, etc. I called it *Hermetic Visits*. It was free of charge and a lot of fun!] They were into bells, crystal bowls, rattles, etc., so I made them a magical rattle that I called The Purple Swan:

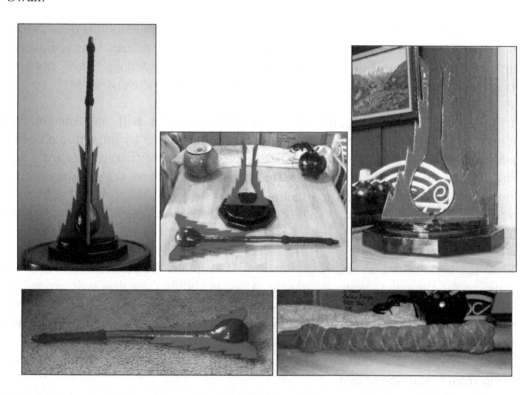

The main body of the rattle was made from an almost perfectly straight Swan's Neck gourd, which I filled (discretely) with very small double-terminated quartz crystals and a lot of quartz bits and pieces. I braided a handle grip with knots at each end, in black suede, and added cardboard flames to the sides. The stand, which is also made entirely out of cardboard, is designed in such a way that one must *carefully* insert and remove the rattle.

A rattle is a handy tool in the appropriate circumstances, especially one filled with quartz crystal. When those quartz bits all bang into each other inside the constraints of the rattle, a piezoelectric charge develops. This charge combines readily with any astra-mental energy one wishes to project or accumulate and gives it a good physical grounding. Besides, it had a really cool rattle sound! Ha!

This was a one-off tool and I haven't ever made another. Although I used to work extensively with gourds in the early 2000's (you can see a couple of examples in the background of the middle photo), this is the only time a made a magical tool out of one.

The Charging Box

The next to the last example of the second class of tools, is the second tool that I made for sale: the Charging Box. [The very first tool I made for sale I'll save for last since its evolution provides a good bridge between the two types or classes of tool.]

Ultimately, this is a very simple tool that does just what the label says – it is for charging things with energies of your choice. It is a basic box with a hinged lid (my very own design), with five double-terminated clear quartz crystals of very high quality, fitted into the top and sides. [The crystals are placed in holes filled with a wonderful substance called Paper Clay which dries hard without too much shrinkage.]

Furthermore, within the body of the box (which is made of three layers of cardboard, covered with stiff card) is a grid of copper wire that forms a sort of

Faraday cage that prevents energies from entering the interior *except through the crystals*. [Laying all the copper wires, a half inch apart, over every square inch of the box was a real pain in the behind! I eventually learned about graphite paint and have since switched to its use exclusively over the copper cage technique!]

Later, I made other models including with just a single crystal:

Whether a single crystal or five, the way this tool works is that one places an object inside the box, closes the lid and then projects whatever energy one chooses into the crystal(s). Because these are double-terminated quartz crystals *and they are pointed inward*, the energy is amplified as it passes through them.

All double-terminated quartz crystals process energy with an inherent directional flow, much like a magnet with its positive and negative poles, and as energy passes through **with** the natural flow, it is automatically amplified to a lesser or greater degree, depending on the individual crystal. Of course I choose crystals that possess a goodly amplifying power! Conversely, when energy is forced through such a crystal **against** the natural flow, the energy is *condensed* instead of amplified. So, theoretically, a Condensing Box could also be constructed by simply reversing the polarity of the crystals.

This is a very handy tool if you're doing a lot of charging things such as amulets, crystals, tinctures, etc. Virtually any energy can be projected into the box: the Vital Energy, the Elements, the Fluids, Adonai Light, or Kethric Brilliance, to name a few. With some models, I "tuned" the side crystals to the Elements and the top crystal to the Kethric Brilliance. [I'll explain "tuning" further on.]

The Tree of Life Meditation Altar

My last example in this class, also aids the magician but in a different sort of way: The Tree of Life Meditation Altar.

This takes us to a totally different chapter of my life: Cloverdale, California, about 75 miles south along the HWY101, at the northern most edge of Sonoma County. The population was about 2-3 times that of Laytonville at the time, so it was quite an urbanization for me, a shock to all my sense! LOL I moved (rather, I was moved *by* a company of very dear friends with trucks and strong arms) in the year 2000, having survived Y2K, into a very nice, single storey, one bedroom apartment in a low-income complex, with lots of closet space and access to my own garden plot, etc.   I really lucked out! In fact I live in the same complex again, now, with a ten year hiatus to Cazadero and Berlin in the middle. It's good to be home although I do miss living in the middle of nowhere!

At any rate, my tool building took a turn in C'dale and I looked to how I could earn some extra money (times were real tight back then) in an ethical way, while in some way enriching the world through my creations. Nothing would ever be assembly-line produced but would instead, be produced individually and magically by my hands alone.

It had to be something inexpensive to make and the only thing that came to mind was something made of cardboard. Cardboard was free; every store in town had a supply of used boxes they wanted to get rid of! And for the thick card I used to cover the cardboard there was cereal box card (I quickly had all my neighbors saving their cereal boxes for me). So I began making decorative "boxes" of all shapes and sizes in order to hone my skills – I knew it had to be better built than my Magic Mirror Box!

Eventually, out of my (somewhat twisted by normal standards) imagination came the Tree of Life Meditation Altar: a beautiful 3-D presentation of the Hebrew and Gra Tree of Life to aid meditation. A not-so-simple object of contemplation for anyone studying Kabbalah.

Each took about two weeks to make, if I remember correctly and sold for $100.00 with free shipping worldwide. The base, gold disk and the cover box are all made with cardboard, covered with cereal box card. The pillars are wood with gold caps made of thick card.

The decorations of the cover box (the gold pentagram and silver heptagram) and the Sephirotic disks on both Trees are cut from thick card (cereal boxes) and painted. The Paths on the two Trees are printed (with my trusty color ink-jet) on 110lb paper stock, then carefully cut out with my handy x-acto knife, and *painstakingly* glued into place individually. The end result is a truly 3-D Tree of Life; the Sephirot jump out in front and each Path strip is independent of the others and crosses on top or underneath in interesting ways that draw the eye and lead the mind on a little journey. And, importantly, they look pretty! Ha!

Since I was planning to make a number of them over time, I wrote down a set of instructions so I wouldn't forget anything and wouldn't have to do all the math again, etc. Here now is the final, revised many times, version of those rather extensive instructions:

Tree of Life Meditation Altar
~ Construction Directions ~
© 2006 by Rawn Clark

8" Diameter Disk —

1) Print path-strip and sephirot pages on 110lb white cardstock and spray with high-gloss lacquer. Print disk pages on 110lb white cardstock but do not spray.

2) Glue disk print-outs to inner side of cereal box cardboard and when dry, trim excess.

3) Glue Gra Tree disk to one side of corrugated cardboard and when dry, trim excess.

4) Glue Hebrew Tree disk to opposite side and press till dry.

5) Glue cereal box cardboard (slick side out) to curved edges and when dry, trim excess.

6) Add glue to exterior of trimmed edge to heal any unevenness.

7) Paint surfaces with Gold (two coats), leaving sephirot unpainted.

8) Glue sephirot print-out to slick side of cereal box cardboard and when dry, use small scissors to trim excess from all 20 sephirot.

9) Pre-cut bottoms and sides of path-strips.

10) Use compass to redefine edges of sephirot circles where path-strip guidelines intersect.

11) Glue path-strips in "creative sequence" to their positions on Gra Tree side of Gold painted disk using watered-down glue.

12) Use compass to redefine edges of sephirot circles where path-strips intersect and trim the overlap.

13) Carefully fit sephirot in place and glue with watered-down glue.

14) Turn over and place on white washcloth to protect finished side and repeat the gluing of path-strips and sephirot to the Hebrew Tree side.

Pillars Caps —

1) Use compass to draw 32 (4x8 layers each cap) 1½" diameter circles, with internal 1" diameter circles, on inner side of Cheerios cereal box cardboard.

2) Use knife to cut out interior circles and small scissors to trim exterior excess on all 32 circles.

3) Using watered-down glue, glue 8 layers together times 4, making sure the layers are closely aligned. Press till dry.

4) Measure, cut and glue thin strips of Cheerios cardboard, slick side in, to edges of all 4 caps and trim any excess when dry.

5) Glue caps (slick side <u>up</u>) to slick side of Cheerios cardboard and when dry, trim excess.

6) Glue caps top-down to 110lb white cardstock and trim outer edge with small scissors when dry. Use knife to cut out interior circle.

7) Paint upper caps Gold (2 coats) on tops, bottoms and sides, and paint lower caps on tops and sides only, leaving their undersides free of paint.

8" Tall Pillars —

1) Measure and cut two 8" sections from a 1" diameter wood dowel.

2) Clamp metal yardstick to table, align pillar and using yardstick as a flat surface, draw straight light down the length of each pillar with pencil.

3) Take one of the 1" diameter cutouts from a pillar cap bisected by a pencil line and place it on the end of the pillar. Align with already established line and mark on opposite side for second line. Mark both ends of both pillars in this way.

4) Realign pillar with yardstick and draw second line in pencil on each pillar as above.

5) Run wide scotch tape along lines to mask <u>white</u> sides of pillars and then paint exposed area with raw black paint (no glue mixed in) — two coats.

6) Remove tape mask and paint the other half with raw white paint — two coats.

3-Tiered Altar Base —

1) Measure and cut from printed (outer) side of corrugated cardboard:
   - 3 @ 2½" x 10½"
   - 3 @ 3½" x 11½"
   - 3 @ 4½" x 12½"

2) Glue two pieces of each tier together and press till dry. When dry, glue third layer to each tier and press till dry.

3) Face sides and tops of each tier with cereal box cardboard (slick side <u>in</u>) and trim excess when dry.

4) Glue each tier top-side down, onto 110lb white cardstock and wrap stock over edges, anchoring on underside. Press tiers till dry and flat.

5) Draw guidelines ½" from edges on the tops of the two lower tiers and glue lower tiers together. Press till dry and then glue top tier in place. Press heavily till dry and flat.

6) Paint tops and sides of base with mixture of black paint and glue (two coats).

7) Glue felt to bottom underside of base and trim excess when dry. Do <u>not</u> press dry!!

Final Assembly of Altar —

      1) Glue pillars to disk:
            a) Lay disk, Gra-face up, on ⅜" wood blocks, making sure it is stable.
            b) With black side facing you, determine most perpendicular side of pillar using an upright angle measure. Then make a small pencil mark, at the meeting of black and white, 2½" up from bottom and 6½" up from bottom.
            c) Apply glue heavily to the left-hand side of Gra-face disk where it will attach to the pillar. Let glue dry slightly and then place disk back down on wood blocks.
            d) Align the pillar, black side up, so that the lower pencil mark meets up with the bottom of the glued disk edge and so the upper mark meets up with the top of the glued disk edge. Make sure that the meeting of black and white aligns with the center of the disk and press together firmly. Measure to see that the pillar is level with the plane of the disk.
            e) When dry, turn over and repeat for opposite pillar.
      2) Attach bottom caps to pillars:
            a) Fit caps to pillars without glue first to make sure they go on easily.
            b) Fill interior of caps with glue and let dry slightly.
            c) Stand Altar up and fit pillar bottoms into caps with glue.
            d) Using a right-angle, make sure the Altar stands true at 90°.
      3) Attach top caps in similar fashion using a right-angle to assure that caps are level.
      4) Set Altar atop base and measure so that it stands in the exact center. Mark position onto base with pencil by outlining lower pillar cap placement.
      5) Apply glue to undersides of lower pillar caps and let dry slightly. Place on base to align perfectly with pencil markings. Press down firmly and remove any excess glue.

Cover Box —

      1) Measure and cut from printed (outer) side of corrugated cardboard:
            2 fronts @ 12-1/2" x 10-5/16"
            2 backs @ 11-7/8" x 10"
            4 sides @ 4-3/16" x 10"
            2 tops @ 12-1/2" x 4-3/16"

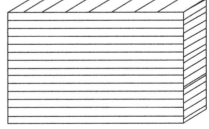

      2) Glue both pieces of front, back, top and both sides together and press till dry and flat.
      3) Paint inner sides of all pieces with raw black (no glue added) paint — one coat — and let dry. Once dry, press overnight to flatten.

4) Apply glue heavily to side edge of back and lay black side up on flat surface. Use book weights to assure flatness and then align side to fit. Use right angle to assure true 90°. When dry, repeat for other side panel.

5) When sides are dry, apply top in same manner.

6) Apply glue heavily to raw edges of sides and top and attach the front panel. Use book weights inside to assure flatness and press till dry.

7) Face all exterior surfaces with cereal box cardboard (slick side <u>in</u>).

8) Face lower raw edge with thin strip of cereal box cardboard, slick side <u>out</u>.

9) When completely dry, spray interior with high-gloss lacquer.

10) Paint exterior top, sides and left-hand sides of front and back with mixture of black paint and glue — two coats. Paint right-hand sides of front and back with mixture of white paint and glue — three coats.

Decorative Elements for Cover Box —

1) Gold trim:
   a) Measure and cut from the <u>inner</u>-side of Cheerios cardboard —
      6 <u>long</u> ⅜" strips
      13 <u>short</u> ⅜" strips
   b) Paint inner-side of all strips Gold (one thick coat).

2) Gold Pentacles:
   a) Using compass, draw two 4½" diameter circles on 110lb white cardstock.
   b) Using protractor and ruler, draw a ⅛" thick pentacle in each circle.
   c) Glue paper to slick-side of cereal box cardboard and when dry, use knife to cut out the pentacles.
   d) Paint Gold (two coats).

3) Silver Heptangles:
   a) Using compass, draw two 4½" diameter circles on 110lb white cardstock.
   b) Using protractor and ruler, draw a ⅛" thick heptangle in each circle.
   c) Glue paper to slick-side of cereal box cardboard and when dry, use knife to cut out the heptangles.
   d) Paint Silver (two coats).

Final Assembly of Cover Box —

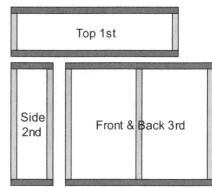

1) Glue Gold trim to Cover Box:
2) Measure and mark guides for Gold (black side) and Silver (white side) stars on front and back of box:

      a) Pent = 2-9/16" down for top mark and 5-11/16" down for bottom mark.

      b) Hept = 2-9/16" down for top mark and 5-10/16" down for bottom mark.

3) Apply watered down glue to back sides of stars and apply carefully — Pentacles centered on black panels and heptangles on white panels.

4) Use ½" measuring guide to mark interior lip at base of box and cut ~2" wide strip of Felt to fit. Add glue to area and apply Felt. Press until moisture is felt through the Felt. Repeat for all four sides of interior lip. When dry, apply glue to bottom of lip and fold the Felt over. Press till moisture is felt through the Felt. Carefully cut Felt at corners so they fit smoothly.

5) When dry, trim excess Felt.

6) With additional Gold paint, touch up the Gold trim at all edges and joints and cover up pencil marks made for centering the four starts.

Final Coating with Spray Lacquer —

When the outdoor temperature is over 60° and the wind is not too brisk, spray the Altar and the Cover Box exterior with a satin-finish lacquer. Let air outdoors for as long as possible and let "cure" for at least 3 days before shipping. [I learned some of my first lessons in international shipping vs. fragility here! I quickly learned that I'd need to pack the hell out of everything in order to get there in one piece! Ha!]

It is really, a simple tool (of the first class) but in its exquisiteness, it has the power to take your mind into the symbolism of either Tree and reveal to you a new, fresh understanding of things. It was fairly popular and in the end I think I made about a dozen of them over the span of a couple years.

Then, the simple little old TOL Meditation Altar started to mutate into something gargantuan and horribly complex! Ha! Ha! It had other incarnations as my cardboard construction abilities matured –

This one had a silk shroud; a small drawer hidden in the front steps; and two hinged doors with depictions of the entire 231 Gates of the Hebrew Tree (in miniature). I think it was 15-16 inches tall and the interior pillars were about 12 inches. This was a one-off tool made for a friend in early spring of 2005.

Then by 2007 I had left C'dale and my comfy apartment with central heat and air and neighbors and cars and noise, and moved to the middle of nowheresville, Cazadero, California . . . well, within 20 or 30 narrow, winding, harrowing miles of bumpy mostly-paved road from downtown. I was living in a small, rustic cabin literally, in the middle of the Redwoods, a good half-mile from the nearest neighbor on over 300 acres of mixed woodland, with a spring and a creek and best of all; I had access to all of it and more! Right outside my front door! It was my version of heaven . . .

THIRD CLASS

My new surroundings inspired me to no end and one of those inspirations became The Gate Maker, which serves as the perfect bridge to a discussion of our third class of magical tool: those that posses an intrinsic power themselves, either native to the material and/or instilled into them by an external force (e.g., a magician), and need a user to activate them. While a magician can certainly convert a second class of tool into a third class by projecting energy, intention, whatever, *into* it, that is not what I'm dealing with here. I'm strictly talking about those tools that from the beginning, contain a specific power or energy, intended to do a specific thing that aids the magician. In the case of the Gate Maker, that aid is to the user's mind in nearly the same way as the TOL Meditation Altar, but this time the mental journey is directed and shaped in specific directions by the magically "tuned" mechanism that is within the Gate Maker . . .

The Gate Maker

I love quartz crystals! No two ways about it! They've always made sense to me and I can see and feel what's happening energetically with them; how they're interacting with their environment. And I've learned *from them* (and other minerals and metals as well) how to take advantage of their energetic properties for use in various kinds of tools. My favorite quartet is quartz and gold, silver and copper wire – with them I can power just about anything! Ha!

So, I had been thinking for a while about making a TOL Meditation Altar that had more oomph, more pizzazz, and that actually aided more directly and powerfully; something that would do some actual work beyond just being an object of contemplation; something that would help *guide* that contemplation. That's what people were really looking for, according to what they were telling me at least.

My answer – The Gate Maker. Over the years, I've made several different *looking* versions but they *all* have had the same mechanism at their heart. **It differs from the TOL Meditation Altar only in that it has small water-clear quartz spheres for each of the Sephirot; and gold, silver and copper wires connecting them for each of the Paths. Furthermore, each of the quartz spheres has been magically "tuned" by me to their corresponding Sephirotic energy (i.e., their Essential Meaning).**

This "mechanism" as I call it, will direct the user and keep them "on the trail", while they explore the Tree. It was designed specifically for use when working the 231 Gates of the Hebrew Tree (and later for the 182 Gates of the Gra Tree) but is also very powerful for general exploration. It would also prove very useful in the practice of The Magic of IHVH-Adonai. All a user needs to do is project energy of any kind into the appropriate spheres (or the whole mechanism) and then transfer their awareness (to whatever degree they are able) into the mechanism and begin exploring.

Of course it had to be beautiful and the astral impact of its appearance had to match its intended use, so here is what I came up with for the very first Gate Maker in 2006-7. [The user manual that follows was written shortly after I made the first one (for the TMO-WG) in 2007.]

The Gate Maker

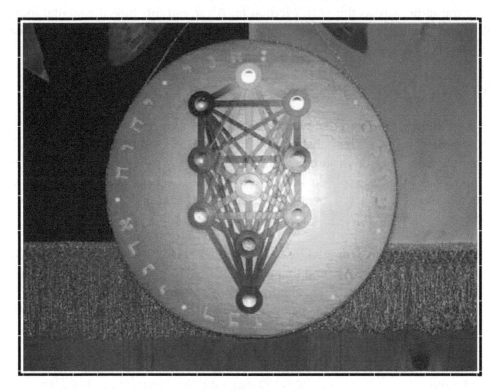

By Rawn Clark
December 2007

The Gate Maker is designed to fulfill only one purpose — to facilitate the exploration / working of the 231 Gates. In this regard, it is unlike any of the other tools I have created for the TMO-WG, each of which can accommodate several different functions. Structurally, it is the simplest of the TMO-WG tools.

Aside from the external decorations (which contribute to its functionality only at the astra-mental level of emotional significance), the working mechanism of **The Gate Maker** is composed of 10 small (7/8 inch diameter), perfectly clear, quartz spheres, connected by strands of (22 gauge) Gold, Silver and Copper wires. The 10 spheres are arrayed in the Tree of Life pattern and the metal wires are inserted in such a way as to form the 22 Lettered and the 16 un-Lettered connections inherent to the Hebrew Tree image.

I've relied upon my usual medium of corrugated cardboard to support this structure of spheres and wire. The main body of **The Gate Maker** consists of a 4 layer thick, 24 inch diameter disk of corrugated cardboard into which I cut 10 holes for the spheres and then incised the 38 connections into the top-most layer.

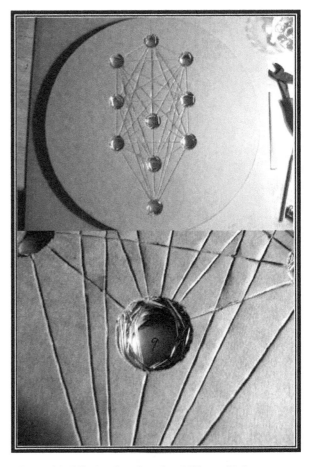

Each connection between the Sephirotic spheres consists of 3 wires which have been carefully laid into the incision. Each wire was cut long enough to have a couple of inches excess to wrap around the interior of each sphere-hole, thus making physical contact with each quartz sphere once inserted.

Three strands of Sterling Silver wire were used for the Pillar of Severity (left-hand side of Binah, Geburah and Hod); three strands of 14k Gold filled wire for the Pillar of Mercy (right-hand side of Chokmah, Gedulah and Netzach); and, a combination Copper, Silver and Gold (one strand of each) was used for the Pillar of Equilibrium (center of Kether, Tiphareth, Yesod and Malkuth).

Each connection originating from the Pillar of Severity is composed of two Silver strands and one strand of the wire that corresponds to the Pillar of its termination. For example, the connection between Binah and Gedulah consists of two Silver and one Gold; and, from Binah to Tiphareth, two Silver and one Copper. Likewise, connections originating from the Pillar of Mercy contain two Gold strands and one strand corresponding to the Pillar of termination. And finally, connections originating from the Pillar of Equilibrium consist of two Copper strands and one strand of its termination Pillar. A complete wiring diagram can be found on the next page.

The wiring of the connections was performed in what I call the "logical sequence". This is a sequential descent from Kether to Malkuth: 1>2, 1>3, 1>4, 1>5, 1>6, 1>7, 1>8, 2>3, 2>4, 2>5, 2>6, 2>8, 2>9, 2>10, 3>4, 3>5, 3>6, 3>7, 3>9, 3>10, 4>5, 4>6, 4>7, 4>9, 4>10, 5>6, 5>8, 5>9, 5>10, 6>7, 6>8, 6>9, 7>8, 7>9, 7>10, 8>9, 8>10, 9>10.

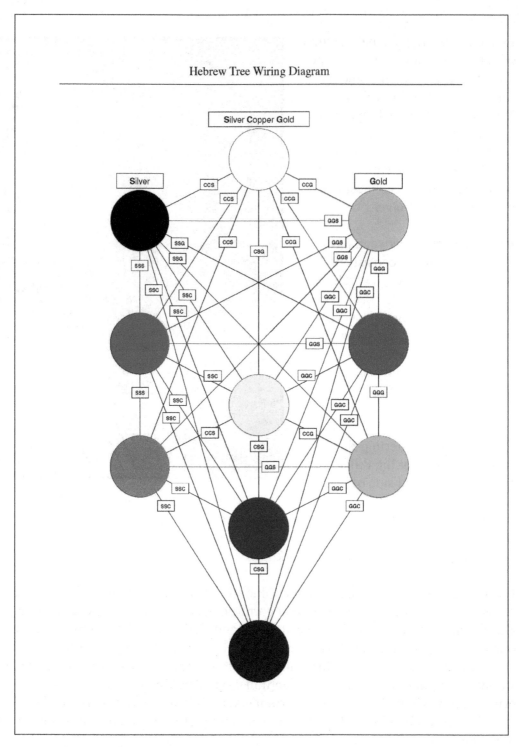

Hebrew Tree Wiring Diagram

Once the wiring was complete, the sphere-hole bottoms were painted with their corresponding colors and the quartz spheres were inserted. Then a prepared disk face of 1/16 inch thick dense cardboard was applied to cover the wiring incisions and secure the spheres in place. Prior to application, the face was painted Gold and the decorative pattern of connecting "Paths" were glued in place. Finally, the small colored Sephirotic disks and Hebrew lettering were applied.

Once the front was complete, the back side was then painted and decorated. The finishing touch was to braid approximately 30 feet of Gold, Copper and Silver wire, which was then wrapped 5 times around the circumference of **The Gate Maker** with an extra loop for hanging.

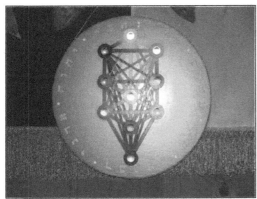 

As you can see from the photo of the front (above), each sphere literally *shines* with its Sephirotic color. :) This effect is due to the fact that a quartz sphere acts as a magnifying lens which directs light upon the focal point, simultaneously illuminating and magnifying whatever is opposite the observer.

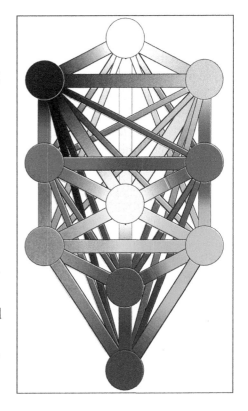

The connecting "Path" decorations are illustrated in the figure directly to the right. This is an accurate depiction which even reflects the "logical sequence" in which they were applied.

The Hebrew text around the edge of the disk (front and back) is, of course, the TMO canticle. On the front, the lettering is painted with a photo-luminescent ("glow-in-the-dark") substance, and on the back, with plain Gold paint.

The back is further decorated with a Hermetic-Kabbalistic motif. The upward-pointing white triangle represents the Universal Principle of Force, and the downward-pointing black triangle, the Universal Principle of Form. At the angles of the triangles you see the three Mother Letters, Aleph, Mem and Shin, painted Gold on the white triangle and Silver on the black triangle.

The hexagon formed within these two interlocking triangles, is painted Gold and decorated by two interlocking, opposing pentagrams. The upward-pointed pentagram is painted red and represents the Electric Fluid and the positive Elements, while the downward-pointed pentagram is painted blue and represents the Magnetic Fluid and the negative Elements.

Once construction was fully completed, **The Gate Maker** was hung in the TMO Temple Room, on the East wall, just above the East Altar and **The Communicator**.

On the night of December 21st, 2007, in true temporal sync with the Sun entering Capricorn (i.e., exact Winter solstice), I charged **The Gate Maker** and "tuned" all 10 of the crystals to their respective Sephirotic essences.

Using The Gate Maker:

Not only is **The Gate Maker** simple in its structure, it's also very simple to operate and use. :) All that is required to "make" a Gate is for the operator to impregnate the relevant Sephirotic spheres with either the Adonai Light or the Kethric Brilliance. Because of the wiring, the connections between Sephirot _automatically_ form once the relevant spheres have been charged. The spheres must be charged in the sequence of the Gate itself. For example, if one is making the Gate of Kether-to-Chokmah, one must first charge the Kether sphere and then the Chokmah sphere.

To "work" or explore the Gate thus formed, one simply projects their astra-mental awareness into the starting sphere and then proceeds to follow the Gate's sequence. [Please note that to "work" a Gate, it is pursued in a "forward" sequence and then a "reverse" sequence.]

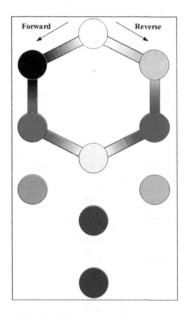

To illustrate, I'll describe the process for "working" the Gate depicted at the right.

Each Gate is "ruled" by its highest Sephirot. In this case, that's Kether which will therefore be the starting point. The "forward" sequence flows down from the highest Sephirot along the connection to the lowest Sephirot. In this case, that's from Kether to Binah. The "reverse" sequence begins therefore, with Kether to Chokmah.

The first task is to charge the relevant spheres. The charging sequence is the "forward" sequence of the Gate itself — first Kether, then Binah, then Geburah, then Tiphareth, then Gedulah, and ending with Chokmah. Formation of the Gate is automatically complete once the final, Chokmah, sphere has been charged.

Once the Gate is formed, "work" is begun by projecting one's awareness into the Kether sphere. This places one within the Kethric Awareness and it is *as* this Kethric Self that one then descends into the Binah sphere and Binah Awareness. Then *as* this combined Kether-Binah Awareness, one descends into the Geburah sphere and Awareness. And so on until one passes through Tiphareth, Gedulah and Chokmah and has reached Kether once again. At which point one then turns around, so to speak, and retraces their steps in reverse order, starting from Kether to Chokmah, to Gedulah and so on, until one has returned all the way back to the starting point of Kether.

The important things in "working" a Gate are: 1) That you *firmly* anchor your awareness within each Sephirotic level as you progress through the Gate sequence; and, 2) That you move as a *cumulative* Awareness (i.e., as a Kether Awareness into Binah, a Kether-Binah Awareness into Geburah, as a Kether-Binah-Geburah Awareness into Tiphareth, etc.). The point is to *thoroughly* integrate the various levels of Awareness involved in a Gate, in the specific sequence of the Gate.

When the entire Gate has been "worked" by travel in *both* the "forward" and "return" sequences, then one is done and must at that point return awareness to its normal physical abode. :) It is important that some time be taken to intentionally integrate the Gate working into one's mundane awareness by mentally reviewing and pondering the experience *before* returning to "normal" activity.

The hexagonal Gate that I've just described can take anywhere between 5 minutes and several hours to "work", depending upon the degree of depth you wish to achieve, the degree of your familiarity with the Sephirotic levels involved, the degree of your facility with the work of shifting your awareness from one level to another, and, well, the amount of time you wish to dedicate to the process. :-) Of the 231 Gates of the Hebrew Tree, there are 38 Lines, 68 Triangles, 74 Quadrangles, 41 Pentangles and 9 Hexangles. Generally speaking, the more complex the Gate, the longer it will take to "work" initially.

My best to you!
 :) Rawn Clark
    28 Dec 2007

Even though I've made a number of different looking versions of the Gate Maker over the years, in *all* of them the mechanism and Path/Sephirot decorations have remained the same with only minor changes in sequence that the Path strips and wires are laid. All told, I made three of this original disk version, one right after another (braiding the wire was a real pain, especially for my fingers!) and then went through a major re-design, mainly because it was very difficult to ship the big disk.

Next came the **Monolith** version (after I had mover to Berlin, Germany for a few years):

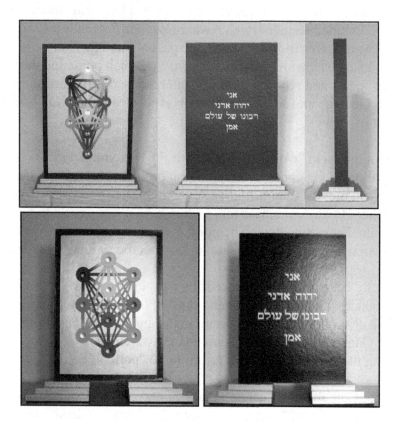

The black structure around the upright rectangular versions *at first* had a half inch grid embedded within (like I described in the Charging Box) until I realized that the energetic of a Gate Maker mechanism is itself isolated and self-contained and didn't need to be protected from external influences in the same way. I made the Monolith version with the Hebrew Tree and the Gra Tree and eventually, even a two-sided version with both Trees. If you look closely at the two types of Trees, you can see that the colored path strips are laid in place in a different order in the Gra Tree Gate Maker (as were the inner wires): this is the "Creative Sequence" which is different from the "Logical Sequence" used in the Hebrew Tree GM's.

Then, masochist that I am (Ha! Not really!), I decided to make it even more difficult for myself and made a few **Cabinet** versions:

I made two of these and they took about two months each to make. Inside the doors was a color depiction of the "Logical Sequence" as it relates to the Hebrew Tree. They stood about 30 inches tall. After making two of them I swore I'd never make another! Ha! Here's an excerpt from the 2009 user manual that came with each Cabinet version to show you how it was made **and also, I describe my all important "tuning" technique:**

Once the wiring is complete, the sphere-hole bottoms are painted with their corresponding colors and a face of 1/16 inch thick dense cardboard is applied to cover the wiring incisions. The face is then painted Gold and the decorative pattern of connecting "Paths" are glued in place.

Then the cabinet enclosure is built *around* **The Gate Maker**. Embedded within the structure of the four layer thick cabinet (including each door) is a half-inch grid of Copper wire which (when the doors are closed) serves to shield **The Gate Maker** mechanism from all external influences. When the construction of the cabinet and doors is complete, they are painted and decorated. The exterior decoration is simple — a gold and violet medallion with the Hebrew Names IHVH and ADNI (glow-in-the-dark coated) from which radiates four violet flames. The inside surfaces of each door are decorated with illustrations of the 48 components of the Hebrew Tree presented in what I term the "logical sequence". Like Hebrew script, they progress from right to left, top to bottom and begin with the right hand door.

When decoration of the cabinet and doors is completed, and construction and painting of the five-tiered base and three-tiered topper is finished, each separate piece is given a thick coating of spray lacquer. Once the lacquer has cured sufficiently, the Quartz spheres are inserted and the decorative Sephirotic disks are glued in place. Due to the design of the door hinges, assembly of the cabinet doors and attachment of the base and topper is the very last step in construction.

In total, *over* 260 hours of labor went into the construction of your **Gate Maker**. :)

Once construction was fully completed, I "tuned" all 10 of the crystals to their respective Sephirotic essences. The tuning process, which takes about 2 hours to complete, begins with the Kether sphere and ends with the Malkuth sphere.

My tuning technique is an aspect of what I call "emulation magic". I begin by filling the Quartz sphere with a very dense accumulation of Kethric Brilliance — this cleanses the sphere and "opens" its physio-astra-mental structure). I then transfer my awareness into the Quartz sphere and **_become_** the chosen Sephirotic state of BEing. This action transforms the Kethric Brilliance (which suffuses the Quartz sphere) into said Sephirotic state of BEing. The end result is that the physio-astra-mental structure of the Quartz sphere is permanently impressed with the essential meaning of the Sephirotic state of BEing. Or, in other words, it is "tuned" to the Sephirotic essence! :)

Since the tuning occurs sequentially from Kether "down", I get to observe the evolution of the physio-astra-mental energetic of the Tree as it "matures" and reaches completion. For example, during the tuning of the Kether sphere, I **_experience_** the seven Kethric emanations to Chokmah, Binah, Gedulah, Geburah, Tiphareth, Netzach and Hod, **_passing through_** the physical wires that connect these spheres in the **Gate Maker**. And after the Kether tuning, I can see that these seven spheres touched by the Kethric emanation are beginning to waken, *already* beginning to manifest their own Sephirotic states of BEing. By the time I turn to the final tuning of the Malkuth sphere, it is already 95% tuned!

Once all ten spheres are tuned, the physio-astra-mental energetic of the Tree stabilizes and becomes a permanent, "locked in" aspect of the physical **Gate Maker**.

Ordinarily, I strongly recommend that all magical tools be covered with silk fabric when not in use, but _this is **not** necessary with **The Gate Maker**_ due to its design. First of all, the Tree, when constructed in this way of Quartz spheres connected by Gold, Silver and Copper wires, becomes a "closed" energy system. In other words, all energies circulate *within* the structure of spheres and wires and are, in effect, "trapped" by this structure. Furthermore, such a structure does not naturally absorb ambient energies from its environment, which means that its environment will generally not affect it. And on top of this, the grid of Copper wire, which is embedded within the cabinet walls and the two doors, absolutely stops any outward radiation of energy from the Tree structure of spheres and wires, thus adding another layer of "closure" to the energy system of **The Gate Maker**.

Even though a silk fabric covering is not required, it's still a nice thing to do. :) If nothing else, it will keep the dust off your **Gate Maker** and reduce the amount of attention it will draw from others.

While your **Gate Maker** is sturdy, it still requires care when handling. Its most vulnerable part is the connection between the cabinet and the 5-tiered base. Since it is constructed of cardboard, care must be taken to **never** get it wet with any liquid, nor expose it to extreme humidity. It should also not be stored in direct sunlight as this will fade the colors.

To energize the photo-luminescent Hebrew lettering (i.e., make them glow in the dark) I recommend using a small flashlight. An LED flashlight is best — mine charges them up n a single slow pass over the letters.

Prior to shipping your **Gate Maker**, I surrounded it with a simple energetic shield designed to protect from extraneous energies during transit. This shield will have automatically dissipated within minutes of your opening the package. :)

Included with your **Gate Maker** is a data-DVD that contains the following: My books, "The 231 Gates of Initiation" and "The 8 Temples Meditation Project", all in Adobe .PDF format; plus, the complete set of nine TMO audio Lessons.

During my time in Berlin I did a lot of experimenting with different construction techniques (it was there that I developed the commercial version of the Radiator, but more on that later), mostly decorative techniques, so I did a few Monoliths with different design motifs on the "back" (or black) side (but I only have photos of this one):

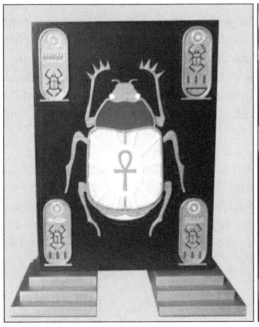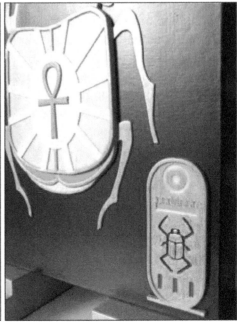

And then, even though I had sworn off braiding three stands of wire forever, I made a specially commissioned piece for a friend, bound in braided wire with a loop hook so it could be hung on his wall:

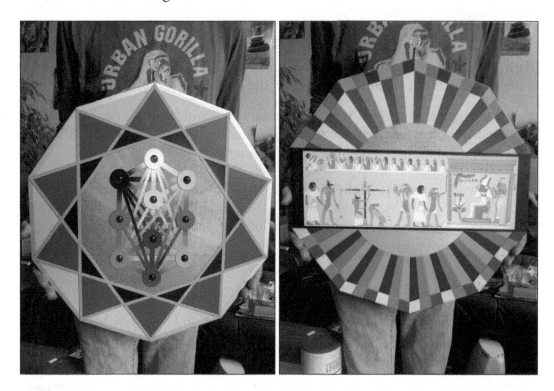

This was some of my finest work and took goddess-only-knows how many hours to make! The solar and lunar half-disks on the "back" side and their rays are actually a mosaic made of painted bits of thick card. The decagon itself is 24 inches in diameter, which is a difficult size to work with, especially to keep several *glued* layers of cardboard drying flat! [Warping is the nemesis of the "cardboardist"! I have to put weights on everything as the glue dries and let it dry thoroughly, and still it's frequently not perfectly flat!]

Not too much later, I moved back to Cloverdale, California from Berlin, Germany after about 6+ years of *BIG* city life. Phew! I actually moved back into an apartment directly across the walkway from my old place, for which I signed a new rental agreement exactly 10 years from the day I left C'dale originally to live in my heaven in the woods! And along with me, the Gate Maker evolved too. Here then is the **Portable Gate Maker**:

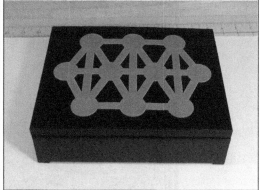

This new version is basically the size of a ream of paper, about 9" x 12" x 2", and it stands upright on the bottom edge. The Hebrew Tree version's about 3" taller. It's the monolith version simplified. This is the version I make exclusively now; it's quick, easy (now, after years of making them!) and less expensive for my customers.

So the Gate Maker in all its incarnations, has served as a crossover into the third class of magical tool (those that possess a power of their own and that require a user to activate its full potential).

The Integrator

For our next example of this class we will have to travel back in time to the first time I lived in C'dale, specifically to late autumn of 2004 and **The Integrator**. This was made for the newly formed TMO-WG. I started work in mid-October and worked for next 49 consecutive days, 8-10 hours each day, and took the final photos on December first.

I'm sharing with you here, the complete user manual that I composed in early 2005 for the TMO-WG members. Although it was written for their eyes alone, the tool itself no longer exists so it's now acceptable to share it publicly. Sadly it died in its final shipping from Berlin across the miles and the borders back to C'dale. The user manual covers its construction and use in detail and is quite long:

The Integrator

By Rawn Clark
October 2004 – January 2005
© 2005

Introduction

It's my pleasure to introduce you to my latest magical creation!   :) This is a
magical tool that I have named *The Integrator* in honor of it's function -- which is
to integrate the awareness' and projected energies of any size group of TMO
practitioners.

The Integrator is, in essence, an homage to both Netzach (Venus) and Binah
(Saturn). Its design is based upon the seven-fold division of the circle which results
in measurements of 51.42857<u>142857</u> degrees. In other words, it's impossible to
draw a *perfect* heptagon — each time one is drawn it is ever so slightly imperfect. :)
Thus *The Integrator* expresses the Mystery of how a sufficient quantity of
imperfection equals perfection . . . seven multiplied by itself, equals 49, which
reduces to 13, the number representing Unity or the perfection of wholeness.

The seven-pointed star of Venus represents the seven planetary Zones or influences which "surround" the Earth and constitute the *human* experience. It also represents the seven colors of light which constitute the full spectrum and the seven days which constitute the week. While none of them is *individually* perfect, the seven influences nonetheless *combine* to create the temporal perfection and this is the essence of ***The Integrator's*** function as a magical tool. ***The Integrator*** serves to combine and unite all of the imperfect individual energies presented to it and thereby produce a holistic energy which is suitable for magical use. This is achieved through the specific structure of ***The Integrator***.

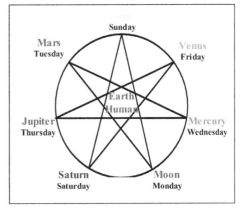

It has 14 sides, representing the positive and negative manifestations of the 7 planetary energies. Each of the 7 planets signified by the 7-pointed star of Venus, is represented by its planetary color to form a 7-hued rainbow. There are 7 tiers of 7, 3-sided drawers, making a total of 49 drawers (a number which is also significant to Binah).

The Integrator is approximately 28 inches tall and 15 inches wide at the base (the drawer area is 13 inches wide). It is constructed of cardboard, paper, Elmer's glue, acrylic paint, lead, copper and spray lacquer. Construction took exactly 49 days (most of them 8-10 hour days!). On the 49th and final day of construction, I sprayed all 49 drawers with lacquer for their protection (the main body was sprayed on day 48). On the 50th day, I photographed ***The Integrator*** and placed it where it will reside in my home.

The Integrator is my personal gift to TMO-WG*ism*. In other words, to all who wish to work TMO *as a group* using this tool. When I die, it will be passed to a reliable individual on the condition that it be preserved for future use and passed on, when the time comes, to other responsible hands.

Photo Gallery

The Integrator sits atop a silk covered round table in the southwest corner of my apartment's living room.

When not in use, **The Integrator** wears its silk Shroud.

When not in use, **The Integrator's** two Spheres and Quartz Wand are kept in their special "box", each wrapped in silk and stored on a shelf immediately below **The Integrator**.

Physical Structure and Energetic Function

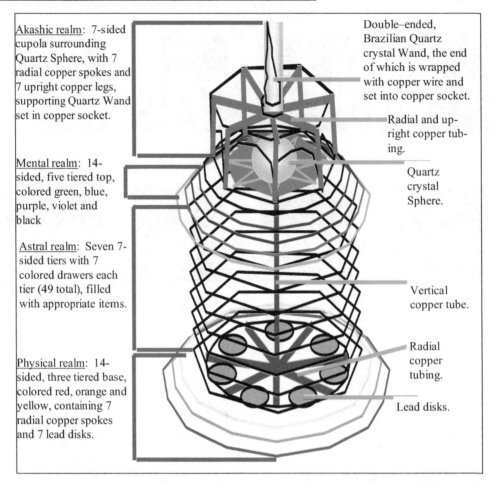

Akashic realm: 7-sided cupola surrounding Quartz Sphere, with 7 radial copper spokes and 7 upright copper legs, supporting Quartz Wand set in copper socket.

Mental realm: 14-sided, five tiered top, colored green, blue, purple, violet and black

Astral realm: Seven 7-sided tiers with 7 colored drawers each tier (49 total), filled with appropriate items.

Physical realm: 14-sided, three tiered base, colored red, orange and yellow, containing 7 radial copper spokes and 7 lead disks.

Double–ended, Brazilian Quartz crystal Wand, the end of which is wrapped with copper wire and set into copper socket.

Radial and up-right copper tubing.

Quartz crystal Sphere.

Vertical copper tube.

Radial copper tubing.

Lead disks.

Physical Realm: The three-tiered base, colored with the lower, red end of the visible spectrum, contains 7 lead disks and 7 radial copper spokes which absorb the physical aspect of any energies presented to *The Integrator*. These energies are all focused upon the hidden vertical copper tube that runs from the joining of the 7 radial spokes, upward through the astral and mental realm portions.

Astral Realm: The seven, 7-sided tiers of seven drawers make for a total of 49 triangular drawers. Each tier contains the full spectrum of seven colors and each set of 7 drawers is off-set to create dynamic motion within the astral realm portion. Each drawer is filled with items corresponding to its color and planetary significance. These items absorb the corresponding aspects of the astral energies presented to *The Integrator*. The triangular shape of each drawer focuses the collected energies upon the central vertical copper tube. Each tier represents, and therefore collects, one aspect of the 7-fold hierarchy of astral energies, all of which are merged within the central copper tube and elevated into the mental portion of *The Integrator*.

Mental Realm: The central vertical copper tube passes through the mental realm portion which is represented by five 14-sided tiers, colored with the higher end of the visible spectrum — green, blue,  purple and violet — and black (to represent the invisible portion of the light spectrum). This portion of *The Integrator* collects the mental aspect of any presented energies and focuses them upon the central copper tube.

Akashic Realm: Atop the mental portion of *The Integrator* sits a 7-sided black platform, decorated with a copper-colored heptagon, at the center of which is a green 7-pointed star. This structure has the effect of condensing all of the collected 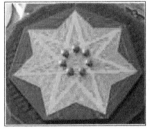  physical, astral and mental energies which have been delivered through the central copper tube. Sitting directly above the top end of the copper tube and supported by 7 small copper-colored knobs, is a Quartz crystal (or Obsidian) Sphere which serves as the receptacle of these combined, upward surging energies.

Surrounding the Quartz Sphere, there stands a 7-sided cupola, each side of which bears a colored emblem composed of a colored heptagon, within which is a copper-colored 7-pointed star and a finer green 7-pointed star. Thus each of the seven faces of the cupola represents the Akashic root of one of the seven planetary realms.

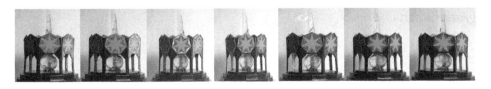

Within the seven supporting legs or pillars of the cupola are individual vertical copper tubes and within the flat top of the cupola are 7 radial copper spokes (which, contrary to what the photo indicates, radiate all the way to the corners of the cupola). At the center top of the cupola is a copper socked into which the Quartz crystal Wand is fitted in such a way that its end touches the radial copper spokes, or atop which one of the two Spheres may be placed.

The cupola therefore creates an electromagnetic field that captures the combined energies emanated by the Sphere which it surrounds, or which are directed into it from below. This field has the effect of amplifying the emanated energy to the point of extreme dynamism.

When an energy enters the cupola structure, the operator may at this point use the cupola to transform the energy before it is either impressed back upon the Sphere that the cupola surrounds, or is directed upward to the copper socket. It is therefore up to the operator to decide whether the cupola will merely intensify, condense and transmit, or if it will also transform the energy which enters into and passes through its specific structure.

When the clear Quartz crystal Wand, for example, is "plugged" into the top copper socket, this amplified and/or transformed energy is condensed and focused in a very tight beam which can then be directed, through the Wand, to any purpose desired by the operator. This configuration of the clear Quartz crystal Sphere below and the clear Quartz Wand "plugged in" above, is only one of *nine* possible configurations of *The Integrator*. There will be instructions for use of each configuration further on, but this primary configuration serves to illustrate the basic function of each of *The Integrator's* parts.

It's here within the Akashic Realm of ***The Integrator*** that the two Spheres and the Wand are employed. Together, nine different working configurations, each with its own unique capabilities, are generated by these three implements.

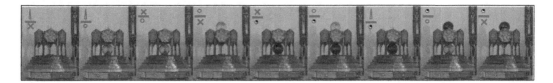

The clear Quartz Sphere:

The Quartz Sphere always serves the functions of <u>condenser</u> and <u>radiator</u>. Its crystalline structure enables it to accept and hold onto any energy projected into it; and furthermore, enables it to radiate any energy projected into it, back out *without* distortion.

Its function is primarily Electric in nature and it is used to manifest the Primordial principle of *Radiance* or Force.

The photo to the right depicts its actual size of 2.5 inches diameter (6.5cm).

The black Obsidian Sphere:

Obsidian is a volcanic glass formed as ejecta cools. It can form in a variety of shades and colors from blues, to reds, browns, grays and, most common of all, a perfect black. ***The Integrator's*** Obsidian Sphere (depicted in actual size at the right) is a perfect black — aside from what is reflected by the glossy surface, it absorbs and holds onto the *full* spectrum of light.

Its function is primarily Magnetic in nature and it is used to manifest the Primordial principle of *Absorption* or Form.

The Brazilian Quartz Wand:

Pictured above (actual size is 6 inches or 15.25cm) is a single Quartz crystal composed of two double-ended crystals that fused together as they grew in the soft clay of their birth. As is common to many Brazilian crystals of this kind, the outer surfaces are all naturally etched and ridged in a random, yet almost hieroglyphic, fashion, while the facets of the tips are clear and smooth.

I wrapped the "base" of the Wand with copper wire in such a way that it plugs into the cupola's copper socket snugly and the "base" of the Wand makes physical contact with the radial copper spokes buried within the cupola.

The Quartz Wand serves an Air or ElectroMagnetically-Neutral function. When positioned by itself with neither Sphere below it, or when it is positioned above the clear Quartz Sphere, the Wand serves as a simple laser-like projector. It transmits and, because of its specific structure and shape, it condenses whatever passes through it into a laser-like beam, but it does not transform or absorb any of what passes through it. In these two configurations, the Wand adopts a primarily Electric function, but when it is placed above the black Obsidian Sphere, it adopts a more Magnetic function and serves as receiver or antenna.

The Shroud: *The Integrator's* Shroud is hand-crafted from black "Raw" silk and a purple "Linen-Look" silk, and is trimmed with a high-quality green wool. The interior is also lined with black "Raw" silk. The Shroud protects *The Integrator* from all physical influences when it's not in use.

The Box: Also hand-crafted (but from cardboard, paint and glue instead of fabric) is the "box" in which The Integrator's two Spheres and Wand are stored when not in use. The Box is 7" by 7" and has 14 sides. The totally black interior has custom fitted nooks for each piece to rest safely wrapped in black silk. The Box is stored directly below *The Integrator*.

Astra-Mental Structure and Functional Awareness

As creator of *The Integrator*, I provided it with an Akashic root cause and conforming to that cause, I provided it a mental body, an astral body and, obviously, a physical body. Thus it is a conscious, magically created entity. Yet even though *The Integrator* is self-aware, it was created to have no will of its own. *It cannot instigate an action of its own volition.* Instead, it must be directed to act by an "operator".

Nonetheless, I designed the specific structure of its mental, astral and physical bodies such that certain limits are placed upon what an "operator" can and cannot do with *The Integrator*. For example, it would be impossible to use *The Integrator* to in any way intentionally cause harm to another. It's not that *The Integrator* would "object" to such a use (it does not possess the capacity for human emotional responses), but rather that it is *constitutionally incapable* of executing such a demand placed by an "operator".

While it is Shrouded, *The Integrator* cannot affect, nor be affected by, its environment at an energetic level. It is however, still aware of itself and its environment even when Shrouded.

When it's "turned on" (i.e., when it has been UnShrouded and any of the three crystals are in place) it is "alive", in the sense that there is *automatically* a self-perpetuating movement of energy, drawn from the environment, into and circulated within *The Integrator* itself. However, it is a very limited aliveness in that it lacks a *directing* awareness. The apparent aliveness is merely the result of its structure -- its action is not personally *willed*, but rather is an automatic response.

Since the consciousness of *The Integrator* is incapable of deciding what energies it will absorb from its environment, it has been given a triple-shield and an Akashic shield. These shields are a permanent part of *The Integrator's* structure and help determine what energies may or may not enter its structure.

The Integrator doesn't become truly alive until an external awareness takes hold of the natural energy dynamic and, through an act of will, directs it to do this or that. When this occurs a discrete entity is formed which is composed of the awareness of the "operator" and the natural energy dynamics inherent to *The Integrator's* structure.

When more than one "operator" is working with *The Integrator*, it will integrate all of the awareness' present into a *single* awareness, directly akin to our WGEs and the TMO-Entity. In fact, *The Integrator* appears to offer the opportunity of merging very concretely with the overall TMO-Entity.

The Ten Rules

Inherent to *The Integrator's* root cause and its overall structure, there are ten "rules" that must be honored.

#1: *The Integrator* will <u>accept</u> only two forms of energy for magical use — a) the Adonai Light *generated through TMO* and b) the Kethric Brilliance. It will not absorb any singular fraction or refraction of Light or any non-holistic energy projected into it. For example, it will not absorb a projection of an Element or Fluid or monochromatic Light. The best for magical use is TMO-generated Adonai Light. The Integrator can <u>transform</u> the Adonai Light or Kethric Brilliance <u>into</u> any energy or Light of the operator's choosing, but it can <u>absorb</u> only projections of Adonai Light and Kethric Brilliance.

#2: *The Integrator* <u>must</u> be cleansed of all non-native or excess energies before and after each use. Prior to use, it should be purged with a simple projection of Kethric Brilliance. After use, the operator (or caretaker) must willfully flush all excess, non-native energy from *The Integrator* and from all crystals that have been used.

#3: *The Integrator* <u>must</u> be kept Shrouded when not in active use. Furthermore, its crystals <u>must</u> be individually wrapped in silk and kept separate from *The Integrator* when not in active use.

#4: A TMO practitioner qualifies as an "operator" for *The Integrator* <u>only</u> after having mastered *at least* Lesson Five of the TMO audio series. An operator's triple-shield <u>must</u> be well established and <u>must</u> be in full force whenever working with *The Integrator*.

#5: *The Integrator* <u>must</u> have a physical, astral, mental *and* Akashic shield in place at all times. The built-in shields may require periodic attention, reinforcement and/or modification.

#6: *The Integrator* <u>must</u> be used <u>only</u> for positive ends. *Always* to help, to create and promote growth, healing and harmony. It <u>cannot</u> be used in any harmful, negative or destructive way.

#7: *The Integrator* <u>must</u> *always* have a steward or caretaker. The caretaker is responsible for keeping *The Integrator* and its crystals clean and safe from harm and prying eyes. The steward is also responsible for keeping *The Integrator* Shrouded when not in use, for UnShrouding it when in use, and for watching over it during use so that it come to no harm.

#8: Since the steward will have to UnShroud, cleanse and ReShroud in order to enable *The Integrator's* use, all use of *The Integrator* by individuals and groups <u>must</u> be negotiated with, and approved by, the steward.

#9: The steward will maintain the contents of *The Integrator's* drawers and will be solely responsible for accepting or refusing any new contents that are submitted.

#10: The very life of *The Integrator* lies in the steward's hands. When the steward becomes unable to sustain their responsibilities over *The Integrator*, they <u>must</u> seek out a new steward, capable and willing to take over, and pass their knowledge on the them. If none can be found then *The Integrator* must either be deactivated or physically destroyed by burning. For safety's sake, instructions pertaining to the destruction, deactivation and reactivation of *The Integrator* will be passed only from steward to steward.

The Nine Configurations and Their Uses

1) The Beacon of Light

In this configuration, where the Quartz Wand is plugged into the cupola socket and there is no Sphere positioned below, *The Integrator* is useful for creating a steady beam of Light. This beam is not particularly suitable for any use other than as an astra-mental beacon which anchors a moment of astra-mental time-space and makes it easier for others to locate. This is very similar to the shaft of Light that arises from the center of the Magic Mirror at our TMO-WG Meeting Place.

Working Method: First the operator must generate an accumulation of Adonai Light by way of TMO. When the accumulation is sufficient, the operator must project it into the body of *The Integrator*, specifically toward the seven tiers of drawers making up the astral region. There will immediately begin a digestion of the Adonai Light within the body of *The Integrator* and a spiral movement of energy through its drawer region will commence.

When the moment feels right to the operator, s/he will willfully direct the digested energy upward and into the structure of the cupola where it will naturally follow the cupola's copper circuitry and become amplified. Again when the time feels right to the operator, he/she will willfully cause the amplified energy to pass into the Quartz Wand plugged into the copper socket, and upward through the Wand so that it emits as a constant laser-like beam of Light.

Once the beam is projecting, the operator will need to replenish the Adonai Light being supplied to *The Integrator*. This means repeating the accumulation of Adonai Light and again projecting it into the body of *The Integrator*. This can

71

either be repeated over and over for as long as the beacon is required or, the operator can perform Final-Form TMO and thus open *The Integrator* to a constant supply-channel of available Adonai Light.

The beam can be stopped by either removing the Quartz Wand from its socket, or by the operator willing the flow of energy to halt.

If the operator wishes to continue with other configurations and work, then any energy remaining within the cupola structure should be willfully directed down into the astral drawer region where it will be re-digested by *The Integrator* and made ready for other uses.

2) Works of Precision and Focused Power

In this configuration, where the Quartz Wand is plugged into the cupola socket *and* the clear Quartz Sphere is positioned below, *The Integrator* is useful for a broad range of mental, astral and/or physical tasks requiring a precise application of the resulting energy. This is likely the most useful configuration *The Integrator* is capable of, since it allows the operator the greatest flexibility in regard to the digestion, amplification and transformation of the Adonai Light.

Most importantly, when the clear Quartz Sphere is placed within the confines of the cupola, it is then possible to perform a "Ribonno Shel Olam" like expansion of the Light focused and condensed within the Quartz Sphere, outward to receive the same sort of blessing as in the practice of TMO itself. This possibility greatly enhances the effectiveness of any work with *The Integrator* since the expansion begins, and the subsequent contraction ends, within the Quartz Sphere <u>before</u> it enters the cupola structure.

This configuration also facilitates the accurate and precise transformation or refraction of the Adonai Light into any aspect that it contains. For example, the condensed and blessed Adonai Light that becomes focused within the Quartz Sphere may then be willfully passed into the cupola structure and there be transformed by instruction from the operator, into any Element, Fluid, monochromatic Light, etc. This "transform" is then sent upward and into the Quartz Wand from which it can be emitted very precisely to the chosen target.

Working Method: The operator begins by projecting a TMO-generated accumulation of Adonai Light into the body of *The Integrator*. When the digestion of the Light meets the operator's satisfaction (i.e., when the time feels right), the operator must willfully direct the energy upward and into the Quartz Sphere where it becomes highly focused and condensed. Here is where, and this is when, the operator must impregnate the condensed Light with its purpose.

At this point the operator has the (recommended) option of expanding the Light contained within the Sphere, outward to the metaphorical "edges" of the infinite Universe in order that it might receive the divine blessing. This is done exactly as in TMO with the Light wave returning to the Quartz Sphere. If the purpose is healing, setting the tone of the temporal moment or achieving a temporal goal, it is then to the operator's advantage to take this opportunity to shepherd the returning wave of Light.

Once the Light has returned in full to the Quartz Sphere, the operator must willfully direct the Light to radiate outward and into the cupola's structure where it is naturally amplified still further.

At this point, the operator has the option of using the structure of the cupola to also transform the Adonai Light into any refraction of their choosing. This is as simple as willfully projecting the command into the cupola that the Adonai Light be transformed into the desired result. Once the command is willed by the operator, *The Integrator* follows suit.

When the transformation of the entire quantity of Light circulating through the cupola is complete, the operator must then willfully direct the transform upward, through the copper socket and into the Quartz Wand. The Wand further condenses the transform and it is then emitted through the Wand and sent to the chosen target.

If, on the other hand, no transformation of the Adonai Light is desired then the Light is merely amplified by the cupola and the operator must then direct it upward and into the copper socket *without* transformation. As before, the Wand further condenses the Adonai Light and the operator then causes it to emit from the Wand and affect the chosen target.

To increase the duration of the emitted beam or to increase its overall strength, the operator must simply project more accumulated Adonai Light into the body of *The Integrator*. And, as noted before, by using Final Form TMO it is possible to establish a continuous flow of Adonai Light into *The Integrator*, and thus produce a continuous emission through the Wand of either the pure Adonai Light or the transform of your choice.

In general, once the process of digestion, condensation, blessing, amplification, transformation (or not) and emission is initiated within *The Integrator*, it will continue unattended so long as *The Integrator* receives more Adonai Light to work with. It will continue until one of three things occur: 1) the operator willfully directs the flow to stop; 2) *The Integrator* runs out of Adonai Light to work with; or, 3) either of the crystals are removed.

If the operator wishes to continue with other operations using this configuration or work with other configurations, then any transform remaining within the cupola structure and the Quartz Wand, should be emitted through the Wand until none remains. **In other words, a transform should never be fed back into *The Integrator*.** Once the transform has been purged, any Adonai Light remaining within the Quartz Sphere (and if no transform was produced, any Adonai Light remaining within the cupola and Wand), should be willfully directed down into the astral drawer region where it will be re-digested by *The Integrator* and made ready for other uses.

3) Softer Works of Radiating or Translocating an Accumulation

In this configuration, where the clear Quartz Sphere is positioned below and the cupola is barren, *The Integrator* is useful for creating dense condensations of the Adonai Light or a transform of the Adonai Light. Since the cupola is bereft of a crystal, it cannot emit (through the Wand) or radiate (through the clear Quartz Sphere) — all it can do when barren is *amplify* and *transform* whatever is presented to it from the Quartz sphere it encloses. This means that once the Adonai Light is sufficiently amplified and/or transformed by the cupola, it must be willfully directed back into the Quartz sphere. The resulting condensate (Adonai Light or a transform) is then radiated or broadcast from the Quartz sphere itself.

This configuration is best suited to accumulations that intend a primarily mental affect. It is not well suited to astral and especially not physical work. While an accumulation *can* be radiated from the Quartz Sphere, the electromagnetic nature of the cupola structure interferes with long distance radiation. In other words, it will accommodate a decent radiation of a few feet (1-2 meters) but will not be effective at any greater distance. For long distance work using this configuration it is most advantageous to mentally transport the accumulation from the Sphere to your chosen (mental) target.

An accumulation generated by this configuration will gently encompass your target, as opposed to forcefully descending upon your target. Its effects will be gentler and therefore more readily/easily digested by your target, but perhaps not as immediately dramatic, when compared to using configuration #2.

Working Method: The operator begins by projecting a TMO-generated accumulation of Adonai Light into the body of *The Integrator*. When the digestion of the Light meets the operator's satisfaction (i.e., when the time feels right), the operator must willfully direct the energy upward and into the Quartz Sphere where it becomes highly focused and condensed. Here is where, and this is when, the operator must impregnate the condensed Light with its purpose.

At this point the operator has the (recommended) option of expanding the Light contained within the Sphere, outward to the metaphorical "edges" of the infinite

Universe in order that it might receive the divine blessing. This is done exactly as in TMO with the Light wave returning to the Quartz Sphere. If the purpose is healing, setting the tone of the temporal moment or achieving a temporal goal, it is then to the operator's advantage to take this opportunity to shepherd the returning wave of Light.

Once the Light has returned in full to the Quartz Sphere, the operator must willfully direct the Light to radiate outward and into the cupola's structure where it is naturally amplified still further.

At this point, the operator has the option of using the structure of the cupola to also transform the Adonai Light into any refraction of their choosing. This is as simple as willfully projecting the command into the cupola that the Adonai Light be transformed into the desired result. Once the command is willed by the operator, *The Integrator* follows suit.

When the transformation of the entire quantity of Light circulating through the cupola is complete, the operator must then willfully direct the transform **back down and into the clear Quartz Sphere**.

If, on the other hand, no transformation of the Adonai Light is desired and the Light is merely amplified by the cupola, the operator must still direct the amplified Light **back down and into the clear Quartz Sphere**.

Once all of the amplified Light or transform is back within the Quartz Sphere, the operator must either willfully command it to radiate outward from the Quartz Sphere or mentally translocate the <u>entire</u> accumulation to their chosen target.

To increase the duration of the radiation or to increase the overall strength of the accumulation, the operator must simply project more accumulated Adonai Light into the body of *The Integrator*. And, as noted before, by using Final Form TMO it is possible to establish a continuous flow of Adonai Light into *The Integrator*, and thus produce a continuous radiation through the Quartz Sphere of either the pure Adonai Light or the transform of your choice.

If the operator wishes to continue with other operations using this configuration or work with other configurations, then any <u>transform</u> remaining within the cupola structure should be passed completely into the Quartz Sphere and should be radiated from the Sphere until <u>none</u> remains. **In other words, a transform should never be fed back into *The Integrator*.** If no transformation was undertaken then any Adonai Light remaining in the cupola should be directed down into the Quartz Sphere and from there, directed down into the astral drawer region of *The Integrator* where it will be re-digested by *The Integrator* and made ready for other uses.

4) Works of General Broadcast or Irradiation

In this configuration, where the clear Quartz Sphere sits atop the copper socket of the cupola and there is no Sphere positioned below, *The Integrator* is useful for creating dense condensations of the Adonai Light or a transform of the Adonai Light and broadcasting them into the immediate environment. This is especially handy for irradiating a room or magical circle with the Adonai Light, Kethric Brilliance, Elements, Fluid, etc..

The one significant drawback with this configuration is that there can be no Ribonno-like expansion of the accumulation after it has entered *The Integrator*. **Such an expansion can only be done with the clear Quartz Sphere <u>below</u> the cupola, sitting immediately atop the mental region and the central copper tube.** Furthermore, the impregnation of the accumulation with your intent should <u>only</u> be done when it is contained within the clear Quartz Sphere and the Sphere is positioned below the cupola. **So with this configuration, the operator <u>must</u> bless and impregnate the Adonai Light with intention <u>before</u> it is projected into the body of The Integrator.**

Working Method: The operator begins by amassing a TMO-generated accumulation of Adonai Light which has been blessed and impregnated with the operator's intention, and then projecting it into the body of *The Integrator*. When the digestion of the Light meets the operator's satisfaction (i.e., when the time feels right), the operator must willfully direct the energy upward and into the cupola structure where it is naturally amplified.

At this point, the operator has the option of using the structure of the cupola to also transform the Adonai Light into any refraction of their choosing. This is as simple as willfully projecting the command into the cupola that the Adonai Light be transformed into the desired result. Once the command is willed by the operator, *The Integrator* follows suit.

When the transformation of the entire quantity of Light circulating through the cupola is complete, the operator must then willfully direct the transform **up, through the copper socket and into the clear Quartz Sphere.**

If, on the other hand, no transformation of the Adonai Light is desired and the Light is merely amplified by the cupola, the operator must still direct the amplified Light **up, through the copper socket and into the clear Quartz Sphere.**

Once all of the amplified Light or transform is within the Quartz Sphere, the operator must then willfully command it to radiate outward from the Quartz Sphere. It is up to the operator to determine what distance this radiation will reach.

To increase the duration of the radiation, the operator must simply project more accumulated Adonai Light into the body of *The Integrator*. And, as noted before, by using Final Form TMO it is possible to establish a continuous flow of Adonai Light into *The Integrator*, and thus produce a continuous radiation through the Quartz Sphere of either the pure Adonai Light or the transform of your choice.

If the operator wishes to continue with other operations using this configuration or work with other configurations, then any <u>transform</u> remaining within the cupola structure should be passed completely into the Quartz Sphere and should be radiated from the Sphere until <u>none</u> remains. **In other words, a transform should never be fed back into *The Integrator*.** If no transformation was undertaken then any Adonai Light remaining in the Sphere and cupola should be directed down into the astral drawer region of *The Integrator* where it will be re-digested by *The Integrator* and made ready for other uses.

5) The Astral Doorway

In this configuration, where the black Obsidian Sphere is positioned below and the cupola is barren, *The Integrator* is useful for creating an astral doorway to any of the Elemental realms or to any aspect of the Earth Zone. The operator (and anyone present) can then mentally or astra-mentally project themselves through the open door and into the desired location. Alternately, instead of projecting through the open door, the operator may evoke an astral entity from the Earth Zone or the Elemental realms, into the open doorway for an astra-mental conversation.

Before I continue describing this configuration, I must say a few things about the black Obsidian Sphere. Where the clear Quartz crystal Sphere *radiates*, the black Obsidian Sphere <u>absorbs</u>. It is incapable of radiation. Its function is purely magnetic. When it is fed a sufficient quantity and intensity of energy, it reaches a critical point at which it becomes very similar to a "black hole" which will form a "worm hole". The intensity and specific vibration of the inward push of energy, combined with the magnetic pull of the Obsidian itself, cause a state where a "tunnel" is bored through the astra-physical matrix, opening a doorway between the target location and the space surrounding the Obsidian Sphere. [With this specific configuration, the doorway is naturally limited to the space encompassed by the cupola.]

In all the configurations involving the Obsidian Sphere, absorption and the creation of a doorway are the primary focus. This means that there is risk to the operator and any other involved while the doorway is open. **It is therefore imperative that whenever working with the Obsidian Sphere, the operator <u>must</u> cast a ritual circle that keeps the doorway confined to a predetermined radius of effect.**

Also, any time the Obsidian Sphere is used, the operator must thoroughly cleanse *The Integrator* and its crystals with a burst of Kethric Brilliance when their work is complete.

[Note: Only those with sufficient experience will be allowed to use this configuration.]

Working Method: The operator begins by casting a ritual circle that will confine the astral doorway should it expand beyond the normal limit of the cupola. The operator then proceeds by amassing a TMO-generated accumulation of Adonai Light (which must be blessed and impregnated with the operator's intention) and then projecting it into the body of *The Integrator*. When the digestion of the Light meets the operator's satisfaction, the operator must willfully direct the energy upward, **consciously and willfully by-passing the black Obsidian Sphere**, and into the cupola structure alone where it is naturally amplified.

At this point, the operator must use the structure of the cupola to transform the Adonai Light into the Element of their choosing, or into the vibration corresponding to a non-Elemental astral target. This is as simple as willfully projecting the command into the cupola that the Adonai Light be transformed into the desired result. Once the command is willed by the operator, *The Integrator* follows suit.

When the transformation of the entire quantity of Light circulating through the cupola is complete, the operator must then willfully direct the transform **down and into the black Obsidian Sphere.**

Once the transform begins to pass into, and be drawn by, the Obsidian Sphere, the operator should immediately resume accumulating the Adonai Light and projecting it into the drawer region of *The Integrator*. This will continue the already established flow of digested Adonai Light into the cupola, its transformation within the cupola and its absorption by the Obsidian Sphere. Feeding of The Integrator should continue until the doorway emerges and becomes sufficiently established.

This doorway, once established, will not need any further feeding to remain open and it will remain open until the operator either commands the door to close, or removes the Obsidian Sphere and cleanses it with a burst of Kethric Brilliance.

While the doorway is kept open, the operator and/or anyone else who is present, may mentally or astra-mentally project their awareness into the Obsidian Sphere and thereby through the doorway, into the targeted astral location.

If the operator desires, s/he may invite any entity they meet during their experience at the astral location, to return with them and manifest to either a mental or astra-mental density within the established doorway. If they consent and do indeed return to inhabit the doorway, the operator <u>must</u> immediately (preferably, <u>immediately before</u> the entity appears) constrict their magic circle so that it very closely surrounds the cupola and restricts the entity to <u>just</u> that area.

As with any evocation, when the work is finished, the operator <u>must</u> direct the visiting guest entity to return to its own realm, escorting it back if necessary. Once the doorway has been vacated, the operator <u>must</u> either willfully command its closure or physically remove the Obsidian Sphere from ***The Integrator*** and cleanse it with a burst of Kethric Brilliance.

After any work with this configuration, the operator <u>must</u> purge the <u>entire</u> body of The Integrator with a prolonged burst of the Kethric Brilliance to assure that absolutely no affects of the astral doorway remain.

6) Spatial Expansion of an Astral Doorway

In this configuration, where the clear Quartz Sphere sits atop the copper socket of the cupola and the black Obsidian Sphere is positioned below, ***The Integrator*** is useful for expanding the (physical) spatial dimensions of an already established astral doorway. By expanding the astral doorway so that it encompasses an entire room, for example, one has in effect relocated the entire room to the astral target, thus negating the need to project through the Obsidian Sphere.

This configuration is also useful for exposing a room and its occupants to the specific influence of the astral target. For example, if the operator wishes to expose a group of participants to the effects of the Fire realm, then a doorway to the realm of the Fire Element would be established and would then be expanded through the clear Quartz Sphere until its dimensions encompassed those present.

And finally, this configuration can be used for evocation of an astral entity to an *astra-physical* density. Not only will this configuration establish the needed doorway through which the entity must enter but it will **also establish the necessary atmosphere which provides the entity's astra-physical sustenance while they are visiting.**

[Note: Only those with sufficient experience will be allowed to use this configuration.]

Working Method: Having cast their ritual circle, the operator is to proceed exactly as in the previous configuration #5 (solitary Obsidian Sphere below and cupola empty) up to the point when the astral doorway has been established.

Once the doorway is well established, the operator must place the (previously cleansed) clear Quartz Sphere atop the copper socked. The Quartz Sphere will automatically begin to resonate with the specific vibration of the open doorway and the operator must then willfully direct the Quartz Sphere to begin radiating the doorway's vibration outward until the desired spatial limit is attained. The operator should then constrict the dimensions of the magic circle until it hugs the doorway's outer limit.

At this point, the operator and any other participants, may move about the astral target or simply absorb the experience of its influence. If any degree of evocation is desired then the operator must proceed as outlined in configuration #5 while taking into consideration the normal methods and special needs involved in an astra-physical evocation.

When work is finished, the operator <u>must</u> shut down *The Integrator* in the following sequence: First, the astral doorway must be shrunk to the limits of the cupola. This is done by physically removing the clear Quartz Sphere from atop the cupola and cleaning it with a burst of Kethric Brilliance. It should then be immediately wrapped in silk. The second step is to extinguish the doorway itself by physically removing the black Obsidian Sphere from its position and also cleansing it with a burst of Kethric Brilliance, followed by wrapping in silk. And finally, the entire body of The Integrator must be cleansed with a sustained burst of Kethric Brilliance.

7) The Mental Doorway

In this configuration, where the clear Quartz Wand is plugged into the copper socket of the cupola and the black Obsidian Sphere is positioned below, *The Integrator* is useful for creating a doorway to the Planetary Zones of the mental realm and for subsequent evocation to a mental density of any inhabitant of the mental realm.

When the clear Quartz Wand is employed above the clear Quartz Sphere, its function is <u>always</u> one of focusing to a laser-like beam and of emitting whatever is fed into it. **But when it is placed above the black Obsidian Sphere, the Sphere's magnetic property takes over and the Wand's function becomes that of an antenna which draws higher vibrational forces and energies <u>into</u> the cupola.**

This provides a necessary augmentation to what *The Integrator* is capable of generating on its own and it is this addition of higher energies and forces into what *The Integrator* provides that enables the formation of a doorway into the <u>sub-Akashic</u> Planetary Zones of the mental realm. **In others word it will establish a doorway to the Zones of Moon, Mercury, Venus, Sol, Mars, Jupiter and the <u>sub-Akashic</u> aspects of Saturn. However, this configuration is not capable of reaching into the Akasha to establish a doorway to the Akashic Binah and the trans-Saturn Zones.**

[Note: Only those with sufficient experience will be allowed to use this configuration.]

Working Method: The operator begins by casting a ritual circle that will confine the mental doorway should it expand beyond the normal limit of the cupola. The operator then proceeds by amassing a TMO-generated accumulation of Adonai Light (which <u>must</u> be blessed and impregnated with the operator's intention) and then projecting it into the body of *The Integrator*. When the digestion of the Light meets the operator's satisfaction, the operator must willfully direct the energy upward, **consciously and willfully by-passing the black Obsidian Sphere**, and into the <u>cupola</u> structure alone where it is naturally amplified.

At this point, the operator must use the structure of the cupola to transform the Adonai Light into the appropriate vibration or colored Light of their choosing, or into the vibration corresponding to a mental plane target. This is as simple as willfully projecting the command into the cupola that the Adonai Light be transformed into the desired result. Once the command is willed by the operator, *The Integrator* follows suit.

At the same time, the operator must willfully direct the Quartz Wand to begin receiving the mental plane equivalent of the transform that is beginning to circulate through the cupola's structure, and to pass what it receives <u>into</u> the cupola. Once the Wand has begun receiving and passing along to the cupola, the operator must willfully direct the Obsidian Sphere to begin absorbing the transform from the cupola.

The operator must continue to feed *The Integrator* with more accumulations of the Adonai Light until the mental doorway is established. Once it is establish, the operator should stop feeding *The Integrator*, at which point the doorway will continue to be refined, purified and elevated by the constant influx from the Quartz Wand.

When the doorway meets the operator's specifications, he/she and any others present may mentally project through the doorway to the mental target. As with configuration #5, the doorway will naturally be confined to the area within the cupola, but even so, the operator should constrict their magic circle so that it immediately surrounds the cupola. And if desired, the operator may evoke a mental realm or Planetary Zone entity to a mental density within the doorway.

When work is finished, the operator <u>must</u> shut down *The Integrator* in the following sequence: First, the mental antenna must be disengaged from the cupola. This is done by physically removing the clear Quartz Wand from the cupola's copper socket and cleansing it with a burst of Kethric Brilliance. It should then be immediately wrapped in silk. The second step is to extinguish the doorway itself by physically removing the black Obsidian Sphere from its position and also cleansing it with a burst of Kethric Brilliance, followed by wrapping in silk. And finally, the entire body of The Integrator must be cleansed with a sustained burst of Kethric Brilliance.

8) Creating an ElectroMagnetic Volt & Opening an Akashic Doorway

In this configuration, where the black Obsidian Sphere sits atop the copper socket of the cupola and the clear Quartz Sphere is positioned below, *The Integrator* affords two uses: a) the ability to create a very powerful ElectroMagnetic Volt; and, b) the ability to open an Akashic doorway through which the operator may work directly within the Akasha itself. Both applications rely upon the polar opposition of functions inherent to the clear Quartz Sphere (Electric, radiant) and the black Obsidian Sphere (Magnetic, absorbent).

When creating a Volt, the operator is working to achieve a dynamic balance of opposing forces (Electric and Magnetic Fluids) within the two Spheres and relies upon their opposing functions (radiation and absorption) to bind these opposing forces together in a self-sustaining embrace. On the other hand, when using this configuration to create an Akashic doorway, only the opposing functions or *archetypal principles* (radiance and absorption) of the two Spheres are employed to initiate the self-sustaining embrace, while the same *unifying* force (Kethric Brilliance) fills them both.

[Note: Only those with sufficient experience will be allowed to use this configuration.]

8a) <u>Creating an ElectroMagnetic Volt</u>

Working Method: Start with configuration #3, where the clear Quartz Sphere is positioned below and the cupola socket is barren.

The operator begins by amassing a TMO-generated accumulation of Adonai Light which has been blessed and impregnated with the operator's intention, and then projecting it into the body of *The Integrator*. When the digestion of the Light meets the operator's satisfaction, the operator must willfully direct the energy upward, **by-passing the clear Quartz Sphere** and into the cupola structure where it is naturally begins to amplify. The operator must then willfully direct the cupola to transform the Adonai Light into the Electric Fluid. When the transformation is complete, the operator must then willfully direct the Electric Fluid down into the Quartz Sphere below.

By repeatedly feeding more Adonai Light into the body of *The Integrator*, the operator must continue filling the Quartz Sphere with the Electric Fluid in this manner until a satisfactory density and dynamism of the accumulated Electric Fluid within the Sphere is achieved. Once the operator is satisfied with the result, feeding of *The Integrator* is halted and all remaining Electric Fluid within the cupola structure is willfully directed into the Quartz Sphere.

At this point, the operator must completely hem in the natural radiance of the Electric Fluid by the Quartz Sphere. This is achieved by willfully directing the Quartz Sphere to inhibit its radiant function and hold onto the Electric Fluid. If successful, the operator should observe that the Electric Fluid within the Quartz Sphere no longer affects the cupola structure and that the cupola remains empty of all energy. Nor does the Electric Fluid feed back down the central copper tube and back into the mental or astral regions of *The Integrator* below. In other words, the Electric Fluid must now exist in very highly concentrated form <u>only</u> within the Quartz Sphere.

Once the Electric part of the Volt has been created and secured, the operator must place the black Obsidian Sphere atop the cupola's copper socket.

The operator begins the second part of the operation by amassing a TMO-generated accumulation of Adonai Light which has been blessed and impregnated with the operator's intention, and then projecting it into the body of *The Integrator*. When the digestion of the Light meets the operator's satisfaction, the operator must willfully direct the energy upward, **by-passing the clear Quartz Sphere** and into the cupola structure where it naturally begins to amplify. The operator must then willfully direct the cupola to transform the Adonai Light into the Magnetic Fluid. When the transformation is complete, the operator must then willfully direct the Magnetic Fluid upward, through the copper socket and into the black Obsidian Sphere above.

By repeatedly feeding more Adonai Light into the body of *The Integrator*, the operator must continue filling the Obsidian Sphere with the Magnetic Fluid in this manner until a satisfactory density and dynamism of the accumulated Magnetic Fluid within the Sphere is achieved. The quantity and dynamism of the Magnetic accumulation must be equal to the accumulation of Electric Fluid residing within the clear Quartz Sphere. Once the operator is satisfied that balance has been achieved, feeding of The Integrator is halted and all remaining Magnetic Fluid within the cupola structure is willfully directed into the Obsidian Sphere.

At this point, the black Obsidian Sphere will be very much like a black hole with an "event horizon" hungry for an influx of the Electric Fluid. If left un-fed, the black hole will close in upon itself and disappear, so the operator must immediately release their restriction of the Quartz Sphere's radiance and allow the Electric Fluid to radiate outward.

For an instant the operator will observe that the Electric Fluid radiates outward from the Quartz Sphere evenly and in all directions, but within a second or two, the Magnetic force of the Obsidian Sphere will draw the entire radiation upward and into itself alone. It will appear as if the Magnetic Fluid completely consumes and covers or obscures the Electric Fluid. Once this occurs, the black hole "tunnels" its way into the core of the Quartz Sphere where the densest part of the accumulation of Electric Fluid is found.

When this tunnel is complete, a continuous, self-perpetuating loop is created and the polar opposite Fluids <u>inseparably</u> embrace each other. This is a true ElectroMagnetic Volt.

Once the Volt has formed, the operator must willfully impress their intention upon it and then send it off to its target (i.e., the Akasha, mental realm, astral realm or physical realm). The act of sending the Volt to its destination is accomplished by willfully directing the Volt to separate from its physical anchor (i.e., from the two Spheres and cupola structure) and then willfully projecting the Volt to its target. Or better yet, the operator can mentally "carry" the Volt to its target.

Once the Volt has been sent and work is complete, the operator must disassemble the configuration and thoroughly cleanse *The Integrator*. Begin by removing the black Obsidian Sphere, cleanse it with a burst of Kethric Brilliance and then wrap it in silk. Then remove the Quartz Sphere and treat it the same by cleansing it with a burst of Kethric Brilliance and wrapping it in silk. Finally, cleanse the entire body of *The Integrator*, including the cupola, with a sustained burst of the Kethric Brilliance. It is best if *The Integrator* is then Shrouded and left to rest for at least 24 hours before being used again.

8b) <u>Creating an Akashic Doorway</u>

Working Method: Start with configuration #3, where the clear Quartz Sphere is positioned below and the cupola is barren.

The operator begins by amassing a TMO-generated accumulation of Adonai Light which has been blessed and impregnated with the operator's intention, and then projecting it into the body of *The Integrator*. When the digestion of the Light meets the operator's satisfaction, the operator must willfully direct the energy upward, **by-passing the clear Quartz Sphere** and into the cupola structure where it is naturally begins to amplify. The operator must then willfully direct the cupola to transform the Adonai Light into the Kethric Brilliance. When the transformation is complete, the operator must then willfully direct the Kethric Brilliance down into the Quartz Sphere below.

By repeatedly feeding more Adonai Light into the body of *The Integrator*, the operator must continue filling the Quartz Sphere with the Kethric Brilliance in this manner until a satisfactory density and dynamism of the accumulated Kethric Brilliance within the Sphere is achieved. As the accumulation intensifies, the operator will observe that the radiant property of the Quartz Sphere becomes stronger and stronger. The goal is to create such an intensity of effect that the Primordial principle of radiance is truly and significantly manifest *through* the Quartz Sphere. Once the operator is satisfied with the result, feeding of **The Integrator** is halted and all remaining Kethric Brilliance within the cupola structure is willfully directed into the Quartz Sphere.

At this point, the operator must completely hem in the natural radiance of the of the Quartz Sphere. This is achieved by willfully directing the Quartz Sphere to inhibit its radiant function and hold onto the Kethric Brilliance. If successful, the operator should observe that the Kethric Brilliance within the Quartz Sphere no longer affects the cupola structure and that the cupola remains empty of all energy. Nor does the Kethric Brilliance feed back down the central copper tube and back into the mental or astral regions of **The Integrator** below. In other words, the Kethric Brilliance and the principle of radiance itself must now exist in very highly concentrated form <u>only</u> within the Quartz Sphere.

Once the radiant principle has been created and secured, the operator must place the black Obsidian Sphere atop the cupola's copper socket.

The operator begins the second part of the operation by amassing a TMO-generated accumulation of Adonai Light which has been blessed and impregnated with the operator's intention, and then projecting it into the body of **The Integrator**. When the digestion of the Light meets the operator's satisfaction, the operator must willfully direct the energy upward, **by-passing the clear Quartz Sphere** and into the cupola structure where it is naturally begins to amplify. The operator must then willfully direct the cupola to transform the Adonai Light into the Kethric Brilliance. When the transformation is complete, the operator must then willfully direct the Kethric Brilliance upward, through the copper socket and into the black Obsidian Sphere above.

By repeatedly feeding more Adonai Light into the body of **The Integrator**, the operator must continue filling the Obsidian Sphere with the Kethric Brilliance in this manner until a satisfactory density and dynamism of the accumulated Kethric Brilliance within the Sphere is achieved. As the accumulation intensifies, the operator will observe that the absorbent property of the Obsidian Sphere becomes stronger and stronger. The goal is to create such an intensity of effect that the Primordial principle of absorbency is truly and significantly manifest *through* the black Obsidian Sphere.

The quantity and dynamism of the Kethric Brilliance accumulation must be made equal to the accumulation of Kethric Brilliance residing within the clear Quartz Sphere. Furthermore, the degree to which the absorptive principle is

manifest within the Obsidian Sphere must equal the degree to which the radiant principle is manifest within the Quartz Sphere. Once the operator is satisfied that balance has been achieved, feeding of *The Integrator* is halted and all remaining Kethric Brilliance within the cupola structure is willfully directed into the Obsidian Sphere.

At this point, the black Obsidian Sphere will be very much like a black hole with an "event horizon" hungry for an influx of the radiant principle. If left un-fed, the black hole will close in upon itself and disappear, so the operator must **immediately** release their restriction of the Quartz Sphere's radiance and allow the Kethric Brilliance to radiate outward.

As soon as the radiant principle is released, it seeks out the absorptive principle and, because of the unifying Kethric Brilliance, a continuous, self-perpetuating loop is created as the polar opposite *principles* embrace each other. The operator will observe that the Kethric Brilliance intensifies to such a degree that it obscures both Spheres and the cupola — as if the two Spheres unite as a single thing, resolving all opposition.

Once this state has been achieved, the operator must willfully cause the Akasha to fill the unified Spheres. This opens a useable doorway to the non-sequential Akasha, through which the operator may project themselves and work directly within the Akasha, or through which they may project a desire, a Volt, etc., into the Akasha.

Once opened, this doorway can also be used to "converse" with any entity one chooses, even a trans-Saturn entity. <u>It must not, however, be used to evoke an entity of any sort, to any density of appearance as there is no way to contain their presence once through the door.</u>

[Note: Evocations can <u>only</u> be performed with the black Obsidian Sphere sitting <u>below</u> the cupola and <u>surrounded by</u> the cupola. Do not ever try to evoke into the Obsidian Sphere when it sits atop the cupola's copper socket. The electromagnetic field naturally produced by the cupola's structural features is harmful to an evoked entity. As a safety precaution, *The Integrator* has been designed to deny any effort to evoke into the Obsidian Sphere when it sits atop the cupola and *The Integrator* will immediately purge itself of all energies present, thus dissolving the doorway. Proximity to such an immediate expulsion of energy from *The Integrator* may have a temporary disorienting effect upon all present.]

Once the work is complete, the operator must disassemble the configuration and thoroughly cleanse *The Integrator*. Begin by dismissing the Akasha and willfully direct the two Spheres to release all of their stored Kethric Brilliance gently into the universe. Then remove the black Obsidian Sphere, cleanse it with a burst of

Kethric Brilliance and then wrap it in silk. Then remove the Quartz Sphere and treat it the same by cleansing it with a burst of Kethric Brilliance and wrapping it in silk. Finally, cleanse the entire body of *The Integrator*, including the cupola, with a sustained burst of the Kethric Brilliance. It is best if *The Integrator* is then Shrouded and left to rest for at least 24 hours before being used again.

9) Rudimentary Magic Mirror

In this configuration, where the black Obsidian Sphere sits alone atop the copper socket of the cupola and no Sphere sits below, *The Integrator* affords only one, rather limited use — that of a rudimentary Magic Mirror.

When sitting atop the cupola by itself in this final configuration, the black Obsidian Sphere should only ever be filled with either the Kethric Brilliance or the Akasha. Either of these will serve to convert the Obsidian Sphere into a rudimentary Magic Mirror suitable only for works of clairsentience, clairvoyance or clairhearing. This Mirror is not suitable for projection or evocation.

Working Methods: a) For an Akasha-based Magic Mirror, the operator simply causes the Akasha to fill the black Obsidian Sphere. **Neither the body of *The Integrator*, nor the cupola are involved in any way.** When the work is finished, the operator must dismiss the Akasha; remove the Obsidian Sphere, cleanse it with a burst of Kethric Brilliance and wrap it in silk.

b) For a Kethric Brilliance-based Magic Mirror, the operator must generate, bless and then project an accumulation of Adonai Light into the body of *The Integrator*. When the digestion is complete, the operator must willfully direct the energy upward and into the cupola where it begins to amplify. Then the operator must willfully direct the cupola to transform the Adonai Light into Kethric Brilliance and feed this transform upward, through the copper socket and into the Obsidian Sphere above. The operator must continue to feed accumulations of the Adonai Light to *The Integrator* until a sufficient density of Kethric Brilliance occupies the Obsidian Sphere.

When work is finished the operator must willfully direct the Obsidian Sphere to release the accumulated Kethric Brilliance to the universe. The Sphere is then removed and wrapped in silk. The operator must then willfully direct any Kethric Brilliance remaining in the cupola structure to descend into the astral drawer region where it will automatically be re-digested and made ready for other uses.

[Note: Evocations can <u>only</u> be performed with the black Obsidian Sphere sitting <u>below</u> the cupola and <u>surrounded by</u> the cupola. Do not ever try to evoke into the

Obsidian Sphere when it sits atop the cupola's copper socket. The electromagnetic field naturally produced by the cupola's structural features is harmful to an evoked entity.]

I tested all nine of The Integrator's configurations and uses in the month after it was finished and this user manual was published to the members of the TMO-WG. Over the span about 12 years it was steadily used by the Working Group and by myself. Over time, all 49 of its drawers were filled to overflowing. The first to go in them was a contribution by one of the WG members: one ounce of each of the 7 planetary metals, all in their pure form (except the Mercury which came in its oxide for safety's sake). Each planet's quantity was divided by 7 and placed in the corresponding drawers. A variety of crystals, some fine gems, small rocks, pieces of metal jewelry, and mementoes of significant moments and places, contributed by many of the members. It was our most versatile tool and the most used (it featured in *all* of our group rituals).

The Unifier

The next in sequence of tools made for the TMO-WG is an extraordinary tool called **The Unifier**. This one has an unassisted effect on its surroundings but it really shines when used by others. Here's its 2005 User Manual:

The Unifier

By Rawn Clark
October-November 2005

Introduction:

The Unifier is a new tool for the exclusive use of the TMO-WG Unity as a whole and for each of the TMO Working Groups individually. The sole function of ***The Unifier*** is to facilitate a unification of awareness among all the participants present, effectively causing the formation of a Working Group Entity and (hopefully) bringing all participants into full conscious awareness **as** the WGE. For each Working Group, ***The Unifier*** will replace the ***Magic Mirror***, (formerly) used as the focal point in the WG's Meeting Place; and for the Unity as a whole, ***The Unifier*** will either be used by itself, or in conjunction with ***The Integrator***.

When used <u>by itself</u>, ***The Unifier*** unites the awareness's of those present and thereby enables the group to function as a single entity which, as we know, exponentially increases the effectiveness and versatility of work. When used in <u>conjunction with</u> ***The Integrator***, ***The Unifier*** eliminates the necessity of each participant projecting their awareness (along with their projection of Adonai Light) into the drawer area of The Integrator, in order to achieve an integration of awareness. ***The Integrator*** can only <u>integrate</u> awareness's; whereas ***The Unifier***, will truly <u>unify</u> awareness's -- which is to say, it will cause a true WG-Entity, while use of ***The Integrator*** alone does not cause this higher state.

When these two tools are used in conjunction, the participants will be able to conduct their work with ***The Integrator*** **as** a WG-Entity.

The Unifier derives its ability to unify awareness's from an Alchemical substance know as the "*Universal Matter*", which was given to me as a gift by an Alchemist friend. From these crystals are derived the Alchemical substances known as *Philosophical Mercury, Sulphur* and *Salt* -- the components of the *Philosopher's Stone*. The primary quality of the *Universal Matter* is that it physically manifests the "*Spiritus Mundi*" -- which is to say the Universal Mind or Life-Force.

It is *aware* <u>and</u> it *emanates*. Its emanation is at all three levels (physical, astral and mental) and the energy it emanates at these levels is *universal* in nature. As it emanates this universalized energy, it encounters no resistance -- which is to say that it finds *commonality* with everything it encounters. Hence its unique quality of facilitating the unification of otherwise separate awareness's.

It's effect upon awareness however, requires a "trigger" to activate. In other words, if you were merely in the same room with it *and weren't aware of its presence and actively thinking about it*, you would never notice its effects. It's as if these faculties within the *Matter* were normally sleeping and awaken only when an awareness brushes against it. And this, of course, makes it ***perfect*** for our needs! :)

Construction:

The structure of The Unifier is intended to focus and amplify the *Universal Matter's* specific property of unifying awareness's. To accomplish this, I have employed the geometry of a 10-sided figure (decagon) and a variety of materials. The decagon represents the 10 Sephirotic Principles and can be drawn in four forms-- representing the Tree of Life in each of the four Kabbalistic "Worlds" (Atziluth, Briah, Yetzirah and Assiah).

Other materials include a basic structure made of cardboard (corrugated and non-corrugated) and glue; various grades of paper; acrylic paints; Copper tubing; Copper, Silver (sterling) and Gold (14k filled) wires; a variety of double-ended Quartz crystals and one Quartz sphere; 10 Fluorite octahedrons; several grains of a Spagyric *Exalted Rosemary Plant Stone* (a gift from a Spagyric "Alchemist" friend); and last but not least, 8" of beard that I cut off at the beginning of September 2005 on the New Moon.

Construction occurred in three phases: the base, the chamber and the top.

The Base

The base is painted black and contains 10 six-ounce lead weights, aligned with the *corners*, for a total of 3.5 lbs (1.6kg). Stationed between each lead disk, pointing inward and aligned with the *flat sides*, are 10 small "wands", each of which is composed of three Copper tubes, bound together by a wrapping of Gold wire and topped by a small Fluorite octahedron (attached with Gold wire). Occupying the center are three double-ended Quartz crystals, oriented to the compass points and bound together with Copper wire. The larger crystal defines the East-West continuum, and the two smaller ones, define North and South individually.

The Chamber

The chamber (which contains the *Universal Matter*) is 5" (12.5cm) tall and is painted a very dark Akashic purple externally and a zinc white internally. Each of the 10 flat sides is pierced with a small hole which has been reinforced by a brass washer, inside and out.

On the floor of the interior, there is a gold-painted geometric cut-out combining all four forms of the decagon, in the center of which is a two-tiered, gold-painted platform to hold the vial of *Universal Matter*.

Centered on each flat side of the purple exterior, there is a silver-painted 10-pointed star with a colored center representing each of the 10 Sephirot. The Sephirotic colors progress counter-clockwise starting with white/Kether in the East. The holes that pierce each side are centered in this colored area.

The chamber is glued to the base, forever enclosing the lead, crystals and "wands" within.

Once the chamber was glued to the base, I began the process of wiring the chamber with (28 gauge, dead soft) 14k Gold (filled) and Sterling Silver (solid) wire. The wiring mimics the geometric cut-out on the floor of the chamber and is anchored at each flat side by passing through the pierced hole and wrapping around a small copper tube on the exterior.

Once I wove the first Gold wire, I noticed that my compass was suddenly registering a 45 degree variance in the magnetic field! ;-) This disturbance of the magnetic field fluctuated between 15 and 62 degrees during the long and delicate wiring process, changing each time a new wire was woven in.

When all the weaving was done, I placed the whole volume of my old beard underneath the wire.

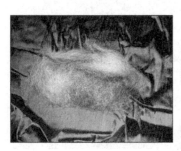  

Then, using Gold wire, I attached 10 small double-ended Quartz crystals (each of which was wrapped with a coil of both Gold and Silver wire) to the woven wires surrounding the place where the *Universal Matter* would sit. Each crystal is aligned so that it points between the *Universal Matter* and the flat sides of the chamber.

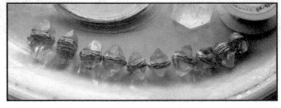

[The wrapped double-ended crystals are shown above with the crystal for Kether on the right and Malkuth on the left.]

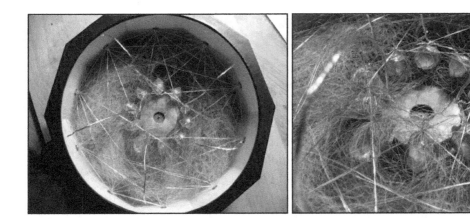

Then came the placement of the vial of *Universal Matter*. Immediately upon placing the vial in its pedestal, the disturbance of the magnetic field diminished to a scant 5 degrees. [It should be noted that I inserted a Copper tube through the pedestal which penetrates into the base and establishes a connection between the crystals below and the vial of *Universal Matter*.]

This was followed by the addition of several grains of Spagyric *Exalted Rosemary Plant Stone* (pictured below, to the left). As I sprinkled the *Stone* over the beard, I was overwhelmed by the most wonderful and intense aroma of Rosemary. :)

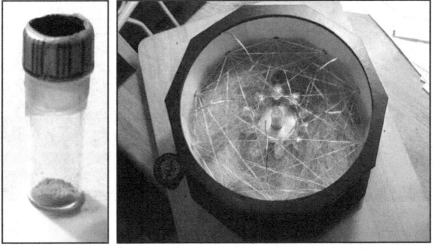

Once the chamber was complete, it was permanently sealed off by the addition of the top.

The Top

The pattern on the top is a variation of the gold-painted cut-out on the floor of the chamber. Here however, the four decagons are drawn one inside the other, with the final, most complex 10-pointed star painted silver instead of gold. At the center of the top there is a hole whereupon will sit the topmost Quartz sphere, along with five much smaller holes through which will be drawn up the ends of the Gold wires that attach the small double-ended crystals to the woven Gold and Silver wires within the chamber.

Once the top was glued in place and the five wires were drawn up through the smaller holes, Copper tubes were slipped over the wires and a pentagonal structure of Copper tubing and Gold wire was built up to secure the Quartz sphere in place

Here then is a photo gallery of the finished piece --

Photo Gallery:

Kether Side

Chokmah Side

Binah Side

Gedulah Side

Geburah Side

Tiphareth Side

Netzach Side

Hod Side

Yesod Side

Malkuth Side

Using *The Unifier*:

The key to using *The Unifier* and to triggering the properties of the *Universal Matter* at its heart is simply to picture the vial of *Universal Matter* hidden within *The Unifier's* chamber. As you visualize the *Universal Matter*, simply allow it to draw your awareness into *The Unifier*. To that end, here are some detail photos of the vial of *Universal Matter* and its placement –

The Unifier may be used by a single individual alone or by a group of individuals. When used by a single individual alone, *The Unifier* will have the effect of automatically unifying all the levels of that person's awareness. A connection with the *Universal Matter* is establish as described above and once their levels of awareness have been unified, the individual may then do what they please __as__ a unified awareness, <u>independent of</u> **The Unifier**. **The Unifier** does not hold onto, constrict nor contain an awareness after unifying it; but rather, it continues to support and maintain the unification until the individual wishes to return to a more "normal" state of consciousness.

When used by a group, **The Unifier** will have the effect of first internally unifying the levels of awareness of each participant and then secondly, of automatically unifying all of the awareness's present into a single WG-Entity. Each participant must individually establish their own connection with the *Universal Matter* as described above. Once the awareness's of all the participants have been unified internally *and* as a group, they may then function __as__ a single WG-Entity <u>independent of</u> **The Unifier**. When the group's work is finished, the unified awareness's are split from each other and from **The Unifier's** influence by simply willing it so.

Other than awareness, *nothing* (i.e., no Light or energy) is projected <u>into</u> **The Unifier**. It is __not__ designed to condense or transmit Light or energy in the way that **The Integrator** is. The __only__ "substance" **The Unifier** is designed to accommodate is <u>awareness</u>.

Care and Maintenance:

The Unifier has been given an Akashic shield to prevent use by anyone wishing to accomplish a negative aim and to prevent anyone other than members of the TMO Unity from using it. Other than this, it requires no additional shielding.

It is cleansed periodically with a burst of Kethric Brilliance and its surface may be cleaned with a damp cloth when needed.

The Unifier belongs to the <u>whole</u> TMO Unity and will be passed into the care of another member upon my death. Until then, it resides *physically* in the North-East corner of my bedroom. *Astra-mentally*, it exists simultaneously within the Temple of Brilliance -- in each of the TMO-WG's Meeting Places and in the North-East corner of the main Temple room, opposite **The Integrator**.

My best to you!
  :) Rawn Clark
    13 November 2005

The most amazing thing about the Unifier was that it enabled the formation of the Working Group Entity! This discovery took our group work to another, much higher and exponentially more effective level!

The Consecrator

I really like making tools that affect the user's awareness and the next one definitely fit in that vein. For the first time, I began working with the more complex geometric forms of the platonic solids; namely, the truncated-icosidodecahedron. There's a mouthful for you! Ha! The result was the largest magical tool I have ever made: **The Consecrator**. It took be the whole of spring 2006 to craft. [Note: The Hebrew Tree was used in the layout of Consecrator.]

The Consecrator
A User Manual
By Rawn Clark
2006

Dedicated to Gabriel, Guardian of the West

INTRODUCTION:

The Consecrator is the fourth in a series of tools created specifically for use by the TMO-WG. It is dedicated to and corresponds to Gabriel, the Quarter Guardian of the West and of the Earth Element, who took a personal interest in its design and construction. I relied heavily upon Gabriel's counsel throughout the creation of The Consecrator and it is thanks to Gabriel's intervention that these *specific* Quartz Crystals (32 in number), the Quartz Sphere, the Obsidian Sphere and the table-stand came into my possession. ☺ And of course, it is thanks to the financial generosity of the TMO-WG members that *all* the material needs were afforded (approximately $700.00 in total)!

As with the three other tools I have created for the TMO-WG (The Communicator, The Integrator and The Unifier), this tool now belongs to the TMO-WG Unity and will be passed on to the care of a responsible member of the Unity upon my death.

The inevitability of The Consecrator became apparent during late Autumn of 2005 and it was at that time that I began a conversation with Gabriel about what was needed in terms of function and design. Its primary function was to be a tool capable of facilitating the creating and focusing of a *very* dense accumulation of the Adonai Light. A secondary function was to be a tool capable of splitting all energies into 32 constituent parts (corresponding to the 32 Paths of Wisdom) and then re-assembling them at the central focal point. And a tertiary function was to be a tool capable of isolating specific aspects out of the 32 and re-assembling those aspects at the focal point as a sort of kabbalistic formula.

While its function was fairly clear, its ultimate structure was not. The primary medium I work with is cardboard and at first I had *no* idea how to structurally engineer something that would hold and focus 32 double-terminated Quartz Crystals upon a central, enclosed focal point! ☺ So during the Winter of 2005-2006, I experimented with the construction of various complex geometric closed-forms, such as the dodecahedron, icosahedron and icosidodecahedron. And then, just before Spring of 2006, I happened upon the *truncated*-icosidodecahedron . . . which has 32 faces! ☺ ☺ ☺ This closed-form is composed of 12 pentagons and 20 hexagons. *Perfect!!!*

Almost immediately after building this form in miniature (compared to The Consecrator) for the first time, an image of the completed Consecrator flashed into my mind. ☺ The details were still a bit blurry but I felt a deep confidence that they would become apparent as I progressed through the construction. Little did I know how many new construction techniques I'd have to teach myself along the way! ☺ ☺ ☺ Those who know me personally will recognize that this sort of challenge is *exactly* my favorite way to spend my time! Creating The Consecrator was a genuine joy, one of the higher highlights of my artistic "career" and, I think, one of my best accomplishments.

I began construction on the morning of March 18th, 2006 and completed construction (including the Silk Shroud and preparation of its permanent place in my home) on June 16th, 2006. I began the charging of its 32 double-terminated Quartz Crystals with their respective aspects of the 32 Paths of Wisdom on the morning of June 20th, 2006 and completed the charging the next evening, June 21st, Summer Solstice 2006.

CONSTRUCTION:

The following materials were all used in the construction of The Consecrator:

- Corrugated Cardboard
- Non-corrugated (thin) Cardboard
- 24lb., 32lb. and 110lb. white paper stock
- Elmer's Glue-All®
- Acrylic Paint (Black, White, Burnt Sienna, Purple and Gold)
- Lead Weights (13lbs. total)
- Copper tubing of various diameters
- 14k Gold-filled 24-guage wire (approx. 200 feet / 4oz.)
- Sterling Silver 24-gauge wire (approx. 150 feet / 3oz.)
- Copper wire of various gauges (approx. 300 feet)
- Paper Clay® (to secure the terminated Crystals within their holes)
- 31 Double-terminated natural Clear Quartz Crystals from a mine in Arkansas, USA [Each crystal was hand-picked to be between 4-2 inches in length and between 5/8 and 7/8 inches diameter.]
- 1 larger, polished, single-terminated Clear Quartz Crystal (from an unknown mine)
- 1 Clear Quartz Crystal Sphere (2.5" diameter)
- 1 Rainbow Obsidian Sphere (2.5" diameter)
- Miscellaneous Double-terminated Quartz Crystals (in the base)
- Synthetic Black Felt (on lip and bottom of base)
- Black Silk Charmeuse fabric (for Shroud and for wrapping the Clear Quartz Sphere)
- Purple Silk Linen fabric (for wall behind The Consecrator)
- Wood Table-Stand (for T.C. to sit atop permanently)
- Lazy-Susan Carousel (a circular turn-table affixed to the top of the Table-Stand) with plywood top and Silk cover (allows us to easily turn T.C. to any angle)
- Rawn's sweat and blood (but no tears . . . and only a *little* blood) ☺
- Spring of 2006 ☺
- Gabriel's influence and counsel ☺
- $700.00 kindly donated by TMO-WG members. ☺

The Consecrator is 24" (61cm) tall and 14" (35.5cm) in diameter.

Here then is a pictorial tour of The Consecrator's construction. Some (or all) of this may seem irrelevant, but do please look through it. It will help you more deeply connect with this tool during use if you have some understanding of it from the inside-out, so to speak. ☺

My first step was to create the truncated-icosidodecahedron form out of corrugated cardboard (left). All the edges were sealed with paper strips (center) and a layer of non-corrugated cardboard was applied to each of the 32 exterior faces (right).

Then ½" diameter holes were drilled through the center of each face and the form was cut open.

The interior was then treated in the same manner as the exterior – the edges were sealed with paper strips (left) and non-corrugated cardboard was applied to all 32 faces (center). Additionally, copper wires were inserted into the crevices between each face, thus forming a copper grid (right).

The crevices were then sealed with paper strips; the edge or lip of each half-form was sealed; the ½" holes were drilled through (left) and then expanded to 1" diameter (center); and finally, the holes were sealed (right).

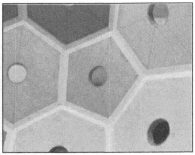

Then the two halves were painted Black on the exterior and White inside.

Once the basic form was complete, I began work on building the 13-tiered, six-sided base. After cutting all the pieces (four layers of corrugated cardboard per each tier), the whole base was hollowed out to accommodate the internal root-like structure. Before putting the tiers together, the edges of each tier were sealed and each tier was painted. Within the hollow, the base was filled with layers of Lead fishing-weights (13 pounds total), to which were attached Copper wire and tubing. Additionally, four double-terminated Quartz Crystals were wired in and all of the wiring was eventually drawn upward to emerge at the top of the base.

Here is the completed base. The base is structured like the roots of a tree which anchor into the soil, thus providing a good "grounding" of The Consecrator's energies.

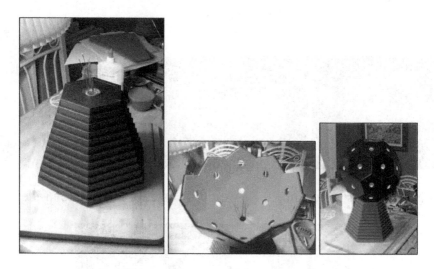

One of the more challenging tasks was the assignment of the 32 faces to the 32 Paths of Wisdom and getting the sequence just right. ☺ I assigned the 10 Sephirot, 3 Mother Letters and 7 Planetary Letters to the 20 hexagonal faces and the 12 Zodiacal Letters to the 12 pentagonal faces, and placed them in a roughly "creative" sequence (i.e., from Kether at the top to Malkuth at the bottom). The 32 Paths of Wisdom correspondence for each face is symbolized by a graphic representation (all of which are explained further on) which was applied to both the inner and outer surface of the face. These graphics were printed on my ink-jet printer onto 110lb card stock and then glued to non-corrugated cardboard. Each was then cut out with an xacto-knife and glued onto its corresponding face. Then the whole form was given a heavy coat of spray lacquer to seal it.

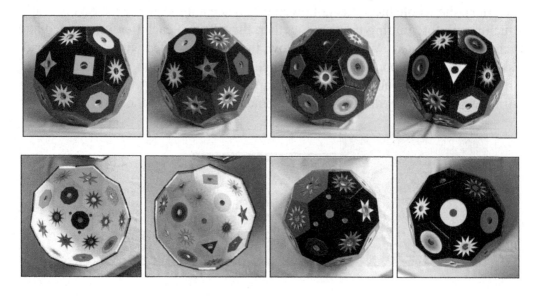

At this point I ordered all the Crystals and Gold and Silver wire. Finding the Crystals was an interesting adventure! ☺ In the end, I ordered them direct from the Coleman Quartz Mine in Arkansas (USA). They were very accommodating and (thanks to Gabriel's intervention) shipped *exactly* what I needed. I was overjoyed at the clarity and perfection of the Crystals when I received their shipment!!! Unfortunately, I never did take any photos of the Crystals themselves. I attribute this oversight to the stress of living with so many powerful Crystals in my home! ☺ ☺ ☺ It was so overtaxing that I had to immediately order a special Obsidian Sphere just to ground out the random energy filling my home!

While waiting for the Crystals to arrive, I took several days to adjust the lip of each half of the form so that they would meet perfectly to form a seal. One down-side of cardboard construction is that it tends to warp a bit and this makes creating one of these closed forms all the more challenging.

Once the Crystals had arrived, I assigned each to one of the 32 Paths of Wisdom and began installing them into their permanent holes. To do this, I used a wonderful product called Paper Clay®, which is a clay-like substance made out of wood fiber instead of silica clay. It air-hardens (i.e., doesn't need to be fired), has a very small shrinkage rate and is no where near as messy to work with as regular clay. ☺ It took two 10-hour days to install all 31 of the double-terminated Crystals. Then I attached the bottom half of the form to the top of the base and installed the final, Malkuth, Crystal (which is not double-terminated).

Again, I'm sorry to say that I took no photos of this phase. ☹ The Obsidian Sphere arrived *after* completing this phase so I was still a bit un-grounded by the presence of so many powerful Crystals!

At last the Obsidian Sphere and the Clear Quartz Sphere arrived, along with my (first) order of Gold and Silver wire, so I began work on the internal platforms that support the central Quartz Sphere (the focal point). I was especially relieved to have the Obsidian Sphere present to ground all those Crystalline energies!!! And it proved a saving grace during the construction of these two platforms! Where it was most useful was during the wrapping of the wire coils around the six legs (3 each for the upper and the lower platforms) that support the platform. Each leg is wrapped with about 26 feet (1/2 oz.) of Copper wire and then by the same amount of Gold wire over the Copper, creating a quite effective electromagnetic coil. Every few minutes during this wrapping process, I had to touch the Obsidian Sphere in order to expel the copious amounts of the Electric Fluid that kept accumulating on my hands! ☺

The two platforms are designed in such a way that when the Quartz Sphere is put in position, it touches Copper wire that is connected to *all* 32 Crystals, thus creating an electromagnetic circuit. It is therefore *through* the Quartz Sphere that the whole is connected.

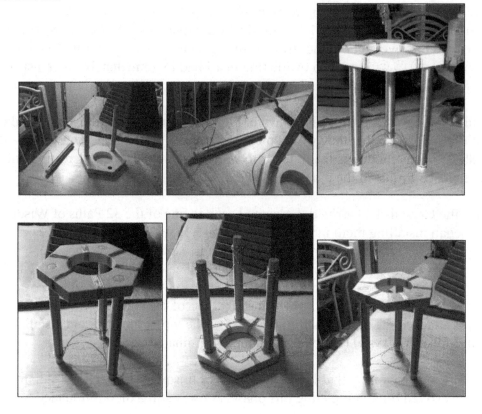

When the two platforms were finished, I glued them into place, fitting the legs into pre-drilled holes.

At about this time, after a month of actively searching, I located (thanks again to Gabriel's intervention) the *perfect* table-stand for The Consecrator to sit atop! I attached a Lazy-Susan turn-table to the top of the table-stand and affixed an hexagonal piece of plywood, covered with Silk, to the turn-table so that we can easily rotate The Consecrator as needed.

Then began the long and difficult process of wiring the double-terminated Crystals together. Twice during this wiring, I ran out of wire and had to quickly order more to continue! ☺ ☺ ☺ All of the Crystals on each half of T.C. are connected to each other externally with 24 gauge Copper wire, Sterling Silver wire and 14k Gold-filled wire. This meant wiring each Crystal three times! ☺ Furthermore, all of the Crystals on each half are wired to the legs of the inner platform (also with Copper, Silver and Gold wire).

Below is a photo of the interior of the bottom half of The Consecrator with the wiring completed:

And the interior of the top half:

With the construction completed, I focused upon making an appropriate space for The Consecrator to live in my home and upon completing the Silk Shroud and holder for the Quartz Crystal (for when it's not in use). This meant rearranging furniture and doing a bit of sewing. ☺

Once I had The Consecrator in place, I placed the Quartz Sphere in position and put the two halves together, creating a complete circuit. *Immediately* I felt the effects of a radiant energy emanating from The Consecrator even though I had not projected any energy into it! With a little experimentation I discovered this energy field has approximately a 3 foot (1 meter) radius of effect which is formed by the energy The Consecrator naturally draws from the ambient environment. [This effect was later confirmed separately by two friends who also felt the radiant energy when standing within 3 feet of T.C..] For this reason, I decided it was wise (and neighborly) to mount a piece of heavy Silk linen on the wall behind The Consecrator to shield my next door neighbor from being affected by T.C.'s presence (especially for when we're actively working with it).

THE CONSECRATOR -- COMPLETED:

What follows is a series of photos of the *completed* Consecrator. Please examine them closely.

Here is The Consecrator, with its Silk Shroud and without it. To the left of T.C., stands one of my best carvings, and to the right, are my best piece of pottery and my best walking stick (which doubles as a magic Staff).

On the small shelf below T.C., there sits the Obsidian Sphere in a special holder (left photo). In the doored cubbyhole below T.C., the Quartz Sphere is stored, wrapped in Silk and sitting in its special holder (middle and right photos). This holder also serves double-duty as a place to set the top half of T.C. when the two parts are apart.

Here is a close-up photo of T.C. in its "default" position with the Tiphareth face (with the yellow hexagon) pointing due East. The Tiphareth face serves as a guide for putting the top and bottom halves of T.C. together properly. Upper-left of the Tiphareth face is the Beth/Saturn face and to the upper-right is the Cheth/Cancer face – these two should *always* straddle the upper point of the Tiphareth face.

Below are photos of each side of The Consecrator's exterior.

Here are photos of the interior of the *top* half of The Consecrator.

And here are photos of the interior of the bottom half of The Consecrator. Please note the Malkuth Crystal directly beneath of Sphere's platform.

And finally, here is close-up photo of the Quartz Sphere. Please note that an occlusion layer near the bottom of the Sphere creates a sort of internal landscape!

THE 32 PATHS OF WISDOM SYMBOLS:

Here is a guide to the symbols I used to represent the 32 Paths of Wisdom --

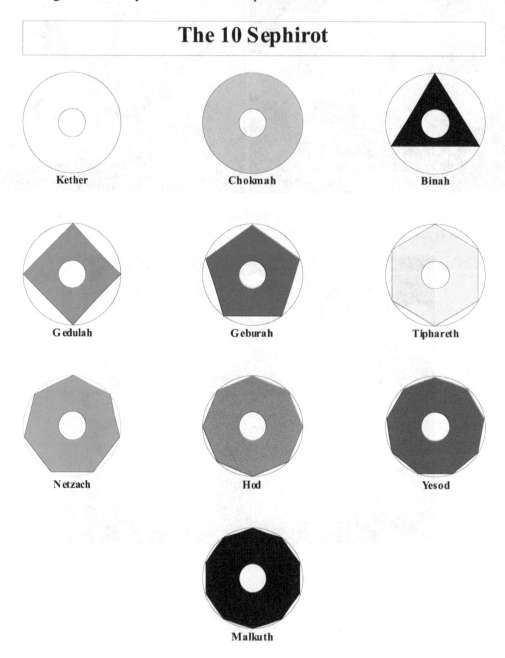

The 10 Sephirot

Kether

Chokmah

Binah

Gedulah

Geburah

Tiphareth

Netzach

Hod

Yesod

Malkuth

The 3 Mothers and the 7 Planets

Shin / Fire
2>3

Aleph / Air
4>5

Mem / Water
7>8

Beth / Saturn
1>6

Gimel / Jupiter
2>4

Daleth / Mars
3>5

Kaph / Venus
4>7

Peh / Mercury
5>8

Resh / Sol
6>9

Tav / Luna
9>10

The 12 Zodiacals

Heh/ Aries
1>2

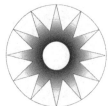

Vav / Taurus
1>3

Zayin / Gemini
2>6

Cheth / Cancer
3>6

Teth / Leo
4>6

Yod / Virgo
5>6

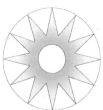

Lamed / Libra
6>7

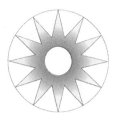

Nun / Scorpio
6>8

Samekh / Sagittarius
7>9

Ayin / Capricorn
8>9

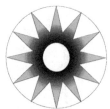

Tzaddi / Aquarius
7>10

Qooph / Pisces
8>10

HOW THE CONSECRATOR WORKS:

The Consecrator is essentially a powerful receiver, amplifier and focuser of energy. Because of the materials used, it receives and amplifies energies of *mental, astral and physical density*. In other words, it takes in the **full** spectrum of **any** energy. The more rarified aspects of an energy are received, amplified and highly focused by the double-terminated Clear Quartz Crystals, while the grosser, more material aspects are received and amplified by the Copper, Silver and Gold wiring, which conducts them into the Crystals.

This is so effective that when the central Quartz Sphere is in place and the circuit complete, *without projecting any energy at The Consecrator*, it will automatically absorb enough ambient energy to generate a 3 foot (1 meter) radius of radiant *physical* energy (which is easily felt)! The entire circuit is grounded through the Malkuth Crystal, which is directly connected to the root-like structure of Copper wire and Lead within the base of The Consecrator.

Because I have charged each of the 32 individual Quartz Crystals with its corresponding Path energetic, The Consecrator is really 32 receivers in one. ☺ Each Crystal receives and transmits (with great purity) its individually designated aspect of any energy, and because of the wiring and the fact that all of the Crystals are aimed at a central focal-point, all 32 aspects are re-combined into a singular energy within the Quartz Sphere. In essence, this exerts an Alchemical "solve et coagula" effect, which purifies and amplifies the energy passing through The Consecrator.

Alternately, if a fine beam of energy is projected at a *single* Crystal, then only that aspect will be received, amplified and focused by The Consecrator. This provides a great amount of versatility in use!

The Quartz Sphere, when placed upon its platform at the focal point and the circuit completed, is the receptacle of all the amplified and focused energies that have been received and processed by The Consecrator. As such, this is the location where most work with the resulting energy is conducted. Through a projection of awareness into the Quartz Sphere, the participants visualize themselves standing atop the inner landscape formed by the occlusion layer and *from there*, they manipulate the energy as desired. It can either be projected toward an external target or the target itself may be visualized as also standing (or floating) within the Sphere in front of the participants and the energy applied directly. From within the Sphere, participants may also draw specific aspects of the whole energy into the Sphere and work with only those aspects while excluding all others.

Alternately, if the participants do _not_ project their awareness's into the Quartz Sphere, a radiant effect is allowed to form and The Consecrator begins to naturally radiate the energy in a spherical shape, from the inside outward. Then, the radiant energy will circulate through The Consecrator in an endless torus-loop as T.C. recycles the self-created sphere of energy surrounding it.

Once the Quartz Sphere is removed from its central platform, *the circuit is severed* and The Consecrator is no longer capable of receiving, amplifying and focusing energy. When standing next to T.C. when it is "turned off" in this manner, one senses absolutely no energetic effect, not even from the presence of so many pretty Crystals. ☺ It's as if *whole* of The Consecrator "hides" when its circuit is severed!

USING THE CONSECRATOR:

Before using The Consecrator a ritual circle **must** be cast astra-mentally to define the working area and to both confine T.C.'s effect and to protect T.C. from unwanted external influences.

To ready The Consecrator for use once the circle is cast, the Silk Shroud must be removed and then the top of The Consecrator separated from the bottom and set aside. Then the Quartz Sphere must be unwrapped and put into place on its internal platform. ***The occlusion layer in the Sphere must sit towards the bottom so that its internal landscape is roughly level.*** At this point the entire body of The Consecrator *and* the Quartz Sphere should be cleansed by a brief blast of Kethric Brilliance. Then the top half of T.C. must be placed back in position to complete the circuit.

Method #1: General Use

With or without the aid of The Integrator, a large and very dense accumulation of the Adonai Light is generated and impregnated with the intention of the working. The Adonai Light is then caused to surround the *entire* body of The Consecrator so that it forms a cloud which covers all 31 of the externally visible Crystals. The Consecrator will automatically begin to draw the Adonai Light inward, collecting it through the 31 Crystals and the Gold, Silver and Copper wires. Most of the Light will pass directly through the Crystals which amplify and focus the Light upon the central Quartz Sphere. The remaining grosser elements of the Light are drawn in by the metal wiring and led directly to the platform, where they are amplified and passed into the central Quartz Sphere (by virtue of the Sphere's direct contact with the Copper wiring of the platform).

Once the cloud of Adonai Light surrounds The Consecrator, all participants will immediately project their awareness's into the Quartz Sphere where they will imagine themselves standing in miniature, as it were, on the Sphere's internal landscape. From this vantage point, the participants will receive the *Consecrated* Adonai Light at the exact focal point of The Consecrator.

When all of the Light has passed through The Consecrator and has collected in the Quartz Sphere, the participants will then visualize that the subject of the working stands or floats (in miniature) within the Sphere directly in front of them. At this point, the Consecrated Adonai Light is applied directly to the subject as desired by the participants.

Alternately, the participants may *project* the Consecrated Adonai Light toward an *external* target, instead of visualizing the target subject as standing within the Sphere.

When the working is complete, the participants will dissolve their visualization of their subject and then withdraw their awareness's from the Quartz Sphere.

The Quartz Sphere is then removed from The Consecrator's interior, cleansed with a brief blast of Kethric Brilliance and then stored below, wrapped in Silk. The top half of The consecrator is replaced and then T.C. is re-covered with its Silk Shroud. And finally, the ritual circle is dissolved.

Method #2: Drawing a Specific Path Energy From the Whole

With or without the aid of The Integrator, a large and very dense accumulation of the Adonai Light is generated and impregnated with the intention of the working. The Adonai Light is then caused to surround the **entire** body of The Consecrator so that it forms a cloud which covers all 31 of the externally visible Crystals.

Once the cloud of Adonai Light surrounds The Consecrator, all participants will immediately project their awareness's into the Quartz Sphere where they will imagine themselves standing in miniature, as it were, on the Sphere's internal landscape. From this vantage point, the participants will draw forth only one of the 32 aspects of the Consecrated Adonai Light to the exact focal point of The Consecrator. ***This specified aspect is drawn directly from its corresponding Crystal.***

When all of the specified aspect of the Light has collected in the Quartz Sphere, the participants will then visualize that the subject of the working stands or floats (in miniature) within the Sphere directly in front of them. At this point, the specified Light is applied directly to the subject as desired by the participants.

Alternately, the participants may *project* the specified Light toward an *external* target, instead of visualizing the target subject as standing within the Sphere.

When the working is complete, the participants will dissolve their visualization of their subject and then withdraw their awareness's from the Quartz Sphere.

The Quartz Sphere is then removed from The Consecrator's interior, cleansed with a brief blast of Kethric Brilliance and then stored below, wrapped in Silk. The top half of The consecrator is replaced and then T.C. is re-covered with its Silk Shroud. And finally, the ritual circle is dissolved.

Method #3: Generating a Specific Path Energy Through a Single Crystal

With or without the aid of The Integrator, a large and very dense accumulation of the Adonai Light is generated and impregnated with the intention of the working. The Adonai Light is then caused to surround <u>only one</u> of the 32 Path Crystals of The Consecrator (or it may be projected into the Crystal as a focused beam).

Once the cloud of Adonai Light has entered the chosen Crystal, all participants will immediately project their awareness's into the Quartz Sphere where they will imagine themselves standing in miniature, as it were, on the Sphere's internal landscape. From this vantage point, the participants will draw forth the <u>single</u> aspect of the Consecrated Adonai Light to the exact focal point of The Consecrator. *This specified aspect is drawn directly from its corresponding Crystal.*

When all of the specified aspect of the Light has collected in the Quartz Sphere, the participants will then visualize that the subject of the working stands or floats (in miniature) within the Sphere directly in front of them. At this point, the specified Light is applied directly to the subject as desired by the participants.

Alternately, the participants may *project* the specified Light toward an *external* target, instead of visualizing the target subject as standing within the Sphere.

When the working is complete, the participants will dissolve their visualization of their subject and then withdraw their awareness's from the Quartz Sphere.

The Quartz Sphere is then removed from The Consecrator's interior, cleansed with a brief blast of Kethric Brilliance and then stored below, wrapped in Silk. The top half of The consecrator is replaced and then T.C. is re-covered with its Silk Shroud. And finally, the ritual circle is dissolved.

Method #4: Drawing a Combination of Specific Path Energies From the Whole

With or without the aid of The Integrator, a large and very dense accumulation of the Adonai Light is generated and impregnated with the intention of the working. The Adonai Light is then caused to surround the ***entire*** body of The Consecrator so that it forms a cloud which covers all 31 of the externally visible Crystals.

Once the cloud of Adonai Light surrounds The Consecrator, all participants will immediately project their awareness's into the Quartz Sphere where they will imagine themselves standing in miniature, as it were, on the Sphere's internal landscape. From this vantage point, the participants will draw forth the first one of the 32 aspects of the Consecrated Adonai Light to be worked with into the exact focal point of The Consecrator. *This specified aspect is drawn directly from its corresponding Crystal.*

Draw **only one aspect at a time** from the whole Light until all of the desired aspects are drawn into the Sphere.

When all of the specified aspects of the Light have collected in the Quartz Sphere, the participants will then visualize that the subject of the working stands or floats (in miniature) within the Sphere directly in front of them. At this point, the *combination* (or formula) of specific aspects of the Light is applied directly to the subject as desired by the participants.

Alternately, the participants may *project* the combined Light toward an *external* target, instead of visualizing the target subject as standing within the Sphere.

When the working is complete, the participants will dissolve their visualization of their subject and then withdraw their awareness's from the Quartz Sphere.

The Quartz Sphere is then removed from The Consecrator's interior, cleansed with a brief blast of Kethric Brilliance and then stored below, wrapped in Silk. The top half of The consecrator is replaced and then T.C. is re-covered with its Silk Shroud. And finally, the ritual circle is dissolved.

Method #5: Generating a Combination of Specific Path Energies Through Multiple Crystals

With or without the aid of The Integrator, a large and very dense accumulation of the Adonai Light is generated and impregnated with the intention of the working. The Adonai Light is then caused to surround (or it may be projected into the Crystal as a focused beam) only the first of the 32 Path Crystals of The Consecrator to be worked with. Work with only one Crystal at a time and repeat the process of surrounding/projecting into each separate Crystal until all of the desired aspects have been energized.

Once the projections of Adonai Light have entered all of the chosen Crystals, all participants will immediately project their awareness's into the Quartz Sphere where they will imagine themselves standing in miniature, as it were, on the Sphere's internal landscape. From this vantage point, the participants will draw forth (in sequence) all of the chosen aspects of the Consecrated Adonai Light to the exact focal point of The Consecrator. *These specified aspects are drawn directly from their corresponding Crystals.*

Draw **only one aspect at a time** until all of the desired aspects are drawn into the Sphere.

When all of the specified aspects of the Light have collected in the Quartz Sphere, the participants will then visualize that the subject of the working stands or floats (in miniature) within the Sphere directly in front of them. At this point, the *combination* (or formula) of specific aspects of the Light is applied directly to the subject as desired by the participants.

Alternately, the participants may *project* the combined Light toward an *external* target, instead of visualizing the target subject as standing within the Sphere.

When the working is complete, the participants will dissolve their visualization of their subject and then withdraw their awareness's from the Quartz Sphere.

The Quartz Sphere is then removed from The Consecrator's interior, cleansed with a brief blast of Kethric Brilliance and then stored below, wrapped in Silk. The top half of The consecrator is replaced and then T.C. is re-covered with its Silk Shroud. And finally, the ritual circle is dissolved.

Method #6: Generating a Radiant Sphere of Adonai Light

With or without the aid of The Integrator, a large and very dense accumulation of the Adonai Light is generated and impregnated with the intention of the working. The Adonai Light is then caused to surround the **entire** body of The Consecrator so that it forms a cloud which covers all 31 of the externally visible Crystals. The Consecrator will automatically begin to draw the Adonai Light inward, collecting it through the 31 Crystals and the Gold, Silver and Copper wires. Most of the Light will pass directly through the Crystals which amplify and focus the Light upon the central Quartz Sphere. The remaining grosser elements of the Light are drawn in by the metal wiring and led directly to the platform, where they are amplified and passed into the central Quartz Sphere (by virtue of the Sphere's direct contact with the Copper wiring of the platform).

Once the whole cloud of Adonai Light is drawn in and processed by The Consecrator, it becomes focused entirely within the central Quartz Sphere in a very dense, radiant state. After a few moments, the whole body of The Consecrator begins to radiate this energy, from the center outward, in the shape of a sphere.

To increase the density, radiant power and/or the circumference of the radiation of the Adonai Light by The Consecrator, the participants should repeat the process of generating a new accumulation of the Adonai Light and then causing it to surround The Consecrator. This may be repeated as many times as desired or needed.

Once the desired size and density is achieved, The Consecrator may be left alone and it will continue radiating this same energy until the circuit is broken (i.e., until the top half is lifted and the Quartz Sphere removed). It is capable of running indefinitely because once the radiant field of energy is established, The Consecrator recycles the energy surrounding it, creating a sort of torus-like continuous digestion of the energy, simultaneously radiating it and drawing it back in to radiate it once more anew.

At no point during the employment of this method should any participant project their awareness into the central Quartz Sphere.

The radiant sphere of Adonai Light formed in this manner may also be separated from the body of The Consecrator and projected elsewhere. This is accomplished through will and visualization.

When the working is complete, the participants will dissolve their visualizations and the Quartz Sphere is then removed from The Consecrator's interior, cleansed with a brief blast of Kethric Brilliance and stored below, wrapped in Silk. The top half of The consecrator is replaced and then T.C. is re-covered with its Silk Shroud. And finally, the ritual circle is dissolved.

Method #7: Generating a Radiant Sphere of a Specific Path Energy Through a Single Crystal

With or without the aid of The Integrator, a large and very dense accumulation of the Adonai Light is generated and impregnated with the intention of the working. The Adonai Light is then caused to surround only one of the 32 Path Crystals of The Consecrator (or it may be projected into the Crystal as a focused beam).

Once the whole cloud of Adonai Light is drawn in and processed by the single Crystal, it becomes focused entirely within the central Quartz Sphere in a very dense, radiant state. After a few moments, the whole body of The Consecrator begins to radiate this energy, from the center outward, in the shape of a sphere.

To increase the density, radiant power and/or the circumference of the radiation of the Adonai Light by The Consecrator, the participants should repeat the process of generating a new accumulation of the Adonai Light and then causing it to surround the single Crystal. This may be repeated as many times as desired or needed.

Once the desired size and density is achieved, The Consecrator may be left alone and it will continue radiating this same energy until the circuit is broken.

At no point during the employment of this method should any participant project their awareness into the central Quartz Sphere.

The radiant sphere of energy formed in this manner may also be separated from the body of The Consecrator and projected elsewhere. This is accomplished through will and visualization. By this method, the practitioner may, for example, project a kabbalistic formula composed of two or more Path energies by first creating the radiant sphere of the first Letter and projecting it into the appropriate realm, and then repeating the process anew for the next Letter, and so on. This allows the practitioner to generate kabbalistic Letters in sequence, one at a time, and to project them individually into different (or even into the same) realms.

When the working is complete, the participants will dissolve their visualizations and the Quartz Sphere is then removed from The Consecrator's interior, cleansed with a brief blast of Kethric Brilliance and stored below, wrapped in Silk. The top half of The consecrator is replaced and then T.C. is re-covered with its Silk Shroud. And finally, the ritual circle is dissolved.

Method #8: Generating a Radiant Sphere of a Combination of Specific Path Energies Through Multiple Crystals

With or without the aid of The Integrator, a large and very dense accumulation of the Adonai Light is generated and impregnated with the intention of the working. The Adonai Light is then caused to surround only one of the 32 Path Crystals of The Consecrator (or it may be projected into the Crystal as a focused beam).

Once the whole cloud of Adonai Light is drawn in and processed by the single Crystal, it becomes focused entirely within the central Quartz Sphere in a very dense, radiant state. After a few moments, the whole body of The Consecrator begins to radiate this energy, from the center outward, in the shape of a sphere.

To increase the density, radiant power and/or the circumference of the radiation of the Adonai Light by The Consecrator, the participants should repeat the process of generating a new accumulation of the Adonai Light and then causing it to surround the single Crystal. This may be repeated as many times as desired or needed.

Once the desired size and density is achieved, the participants should repeat the process with their next specific Path Crystal, by generating another accumulation of the Adonai Light and focusing it upon the next Crystal in sequence. This is repeated with the same Crystal until the desired effect is achieved with the new Path energy.

The entire process is repeated for each specific Path energy, one at a time, until all the desired Path energies are combined together and radiating as a sphere.

At no point during the employment of this method should any participant project their awareness into the central Quartz Sphere.

The radiant sphere of energy formed in this manner may also be separated from the body of The Consecrator and projected elsewhere. This is accomplished through will and visualization.

When the working is complete, the participants will dissolve their visualizations and the Quartz Sphere is then removed from The Consecrator's interior, cleansed with a brief blast of Kethric Brilliance and stored below, wrapped in Silk. The top half of The consecrator is replaced and then T.C. is re-covered with its Silk Shroud. And finally, the ritual circle is dissolved.

Method #9: Wandering the Planetary Zones and the Infinite-Mirror Effect

[This technique enables the participants to use The Consecrator as a vehicle of sorts in order to transit from one Planetary Zone to the next. To begin the wandering, the participants must first use The Consecrator to transit to Malkuth and after arriving in the Earth-Girdling Zone, T.C. is used once again to transit to the Lunar Zone., etc., one Zone at a time in sequence.]

With or without the aid of The Integrator, a large and very dense accumulation of the Adonai Light is generated and impregnated with the intention of creating the vibration of the Earth-Girdling Zone (Malkuth) within the central Quartz Sphere. The Adonai Light is then caused to surround only the **Tav** and **Malkuth** Path Crystals of The Consecrator.

Once the whole cloud of Adonai Light is drawn in and processed by these two Crystals, it becomes focused entirely within the central Quartz Sphere in a very dense, radiant state. At this point, the participants will project their awareness's into the central Quartz Sphere, anchoring the Earth-Girdling Zone energy/Light within the Sphere and halting its outward radiation. The participants now stand in Malkuth, the Earth-Girdling Zone.

The participants may explore this Zone as desired or wander on to the Lunar Zone. To reach the Lunar Zone, the participants must "call" The Consecrator into the Earth-Girdling Zone by willing it to appear before them within the Quartz Sphere. **[In the same way that two mirrors can be set in such a relationship that they infinitely reflect each other, The Consecrator can be "called" into itself an infinite number of times in sequence, each time creating a new iteration of itself. I call this the "infinite-mirror effect".]**

Once The Consecrator stands before the participants within the central Quartz Sphere (which has become the Earth-Girdling Zone), the participants must generate a new accumulation of the Adonai Light (*from within the Earth-Girdling Zone*) and impregnate it with the intention of creating the vibration of the Lunar Zone (Yesod) within the central Quartz Sphere *of the version of T.C. that stands before*

them in the Earth-Girdling Zone. The Adonai Light is then caused to surround <u>only</u> the **Resh** and **Yesod** Path Crystals of The Consecrator.

Once the whole cloud of Adonai Light is drawn in and processed by these two Crystals, it becomes focused entirely within the central Quartz Sphere in a very dense, radiant state. At this point, the participants will project their awareness's into the central Quartz Sphere ***of the version of T.C. that stands before them in the Earth-Girdling Zone***, anchoring the Lunar Zone energy/Light within the Sphere and halting its outward radiation. The participants now stand in Yesod, the Lunar Zone.

The participants may explore this Zone as desired or wander on to the Mercury Zone. To reach the next Zone, the participants must "call" The Consecrator as before, into the Lunar Zone by willing it to appear before them within the Quartz Sphere. The same process is used each time transit to the next successive Zone is desired.

The Formulas for the Zones are:
Malkuth / Earth-Girdling Zone = Tav + Malkuth
Yesod / Lunar Zone = Resh + Yesod
Hod / Mercury Zone = Peh + Hod
Netzach / Venus Zone = Kaph + Netzach
Tiphareth / Sun Zone = Beth + Tiphareth
Geburah / Mars Zone = Daleth + Geburah
Gedulah / Jupiter Zone = Gimel + Gedulah
Binah / Saturn Zone = Vav + Shin + Binah [Note that this is a triple formula.]

In order to <u>descend</u> through the Zones (i.e., return to normal awareness) participants must separate their awareness's from the Quartz Sphere which holds the Zone they presently inhabit. For example, to transit back to Malkuth from Yesod, the participants must exit the Quartz Sphere that is filled with the Lunar Zone vibration, in order to once again stand within the first Quartz Sphere that is still filled with the vibration of the Earth-Girdling Zone (Malkuth). At that point, the participants will be standing around The Consecrator ***within the Earth-Girdling Zone.*** The visualization of The Consecrator that was "called" into the Earth-Girdling Zone Sphere earlier, is dissolved and then the participants separate their awareness's from the Sphere that is filled with the Earth-Girdling Zone, thus completing their transition back to normal awareness.

When the working is complete, the Quartz Sphere is then removed from The Consecrator's interior, cleansed with a brief blast of Kethric Brilliance and stored below, wrapped in Silk. The top half of The consecrator is replaced and then T.C. is re-covered with its Silk Shroud. And finally, the ritual circle is dissolved.

124

Method #10: Self-Purification and Self-Radiance

[This technique may be used either individually, or by a group of participants, and involves the combined use of The Unifier, The Integrator and The Consecrator.]

Begin by unifying your awareness with The Unifier. If a group is involved then all participants must unite *together* and form a WGE. Next, generate a large and very dense accumulation of the Adonai Light and project the accumulation, ***along with*** your (or the group's) unified awareness, into The Integrator (set up in configuration #2). **Your awareness <u>must</u> be merged with the Light as it is processed by T.I..** When your awareness and the Light arise into T.I.'s Quartz Sphere, send it out for the "ribbono" **without** any sort of impregnation of intention. Upon return to the Sphere, rise up with the Light into the Cupola for amplification and then up into the wand, from where you and the Light project to The Consecrator.

Form a cloud which surrounds the entire body of The Consecrator and let yourself and the Light be drawn into T.C. through all of the Crystals and wiring. This will separate your awareness and the Light into its 32 constituent parts and re-assemble them all within the central Quartz Sphere, exercising a purifying "solve et coagula" effect upon your awareness (or upon the group awareness as a whole).

Once your awareness and the Light have been focused within the Quartz Sphere you will gradually become radiant and your radius of radiation will expand to encompass the whole body of The Consecrator. When this occurs, the torus-effect of T.C. takes over and you become involved in an endless loop of self-radiance and self-re-absorption. In Alchemical terms this is called "digestion" which in time results in a comprehensive purification of the matter.

This elicits a very comforting state of pure, radiant BEing. To exit this state, simply separate your awareness from the Quartz Sphere and then break the circuit in the usual manner by removing the Quartz Sphere from The Consecrator.

....

When finished, the Quartz Sphere is then cleansed with a brief blast of Kethric Brilliance and stored below, wrapped in Silk. The top half of The consecrator is replaced and then T.C. is re-covered with its Silk Shroud. And finally, the ritual circle is dissolved.

The Consecrator was a *very* cherished tool and I have a soft spot in my heart for it. Unfortunately, its many travels finally took their toll and in the shipping this last time (from Berlin back to C'dale) it was destroyed. I was able to save all the crystals though (at that size they're pretty indestructible) and eventually made use of them in my second Golem (but more on that later).

The Violet Star

In 2017 I did try to replicate the Consecrator in a much smaller size of about 8" but it was ultimately a failure so I discontinued it and took the original apart to re-use the crystals (in my first Golem). Here then are some photos of my only failed tool, the **Violet Star**:

The failure was in the way that the wires from the crystals all made contact with the central sphere. It proved to be a hit and miss connection (which is never good in a magical tool), and when it did hit, it was nowhere near as potent as its predecessor. At least it was moderately pretty! Ha!

FOURTH CLASS

Now we will have to time travel forward from the Consecrator (made in spring 2006 @ C'dale) to my little cabin in the woods and the autumn of 2007 when I made a special tool as a gift for a dear friend. This tool is of the fourth class and of the type that continuously performs a magical task exclusively by itself, without any involvement by a user (except uncovering it).

The Radiator

Since moving to Berlin, I have made a total of 30 Radiators for people from all over the world! The one pictured below, is the very first Radiator ever (or "Grandfather Radiator" as I've come to call him). His dimensions are 12" x 12" x 16".

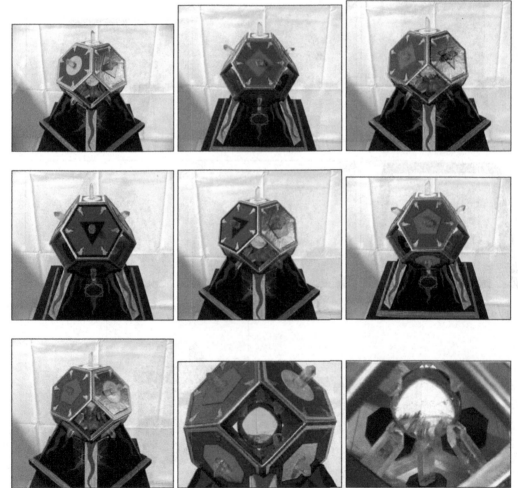

This is the most precise and elaborate bit of cardboard construction I have ever produced; so precise that the inner lid forms a vacuum! It took me 3 months to build but these days, I can build a Radiator in about 2-3 weeks! It has spawned 29 more of its kind in the years since.

It's in what I call the "mechanism" that all the magic happens so here's a little snippet I wrote in 2018 explaining what I mean:

....

The Radiator mechanism automatically generates and radiates a continuous stream of Kethric Brilliance which, when enclosed within a magical Circle, becomes so dense and so intense it can easily be perceived by the uninitiated and those who are normally insensitive to subtle energies. The strength of this radiant effect is the result of the Radiator's physical structure in conjunction with the physio-astra-mental tuning of its quartz components.

The basic shape of the Radiator mechanism is a 'truncated octahedron' -- a 14 sided geometric solid composed of 8 hexagons and 6 squares. Ten sides are each pierced by a double-terminated clear quartz crystal and four sides are completely empty. Each of these double-terminated quartz crystals physically touches a central clear quartz sphere and together they suspend this sphere at the exact center point of the mechanism.

This physical structure alone, without any tuning of the quartz crystals, will automatically draw a modest amount of ambient energy into the central sphere and radiate it outward, but this energy will be of low quality for magical work and of insufficient quantity for any important tasks. When the crystals are tuned however, the quantity of energy generated is many, many magnitudes greater and the quality is rendered suitable for all magical operations no matter how sublime.

The Radiator's 10 double-terminated quartz crystals are each tuned to the essential meaning of one of the Kabbalistic Tree of Life's Sephirot, specifically to the Sephirot of the Gra Tree of Life pattern, and the central quartz sphere is tuned to the Kethric Brilliance itself (the most sublime magical 'energy'). By tuning the crystals in this way, the Radiator becomes capable of generating a continuous stream of the Kethric Brilliance which can then be employed as the magician wishes.

Using a Radiator is quite simple. Remove the mechanism from its containment vessel, re-close the vessel and place the mechanism on the top-most stand. The Radiator begins working immediately upon its removal from the containment vessel.

The mechanism's default position is with the white Kether crystal up and the yellow Tiphareth crystal pointing toward the east. One can however, place the mechanism in any orientation one desires and thus emphasize the upward pointing crystal's energy.

To turn the Radiator off, simply return the mechanism to its containment vessel.

....

So this tool radiates the Kethric Brilliance *continuously*, even when closed up in its container. In other words, the container is only there to effectively "turn off" the Radiator, or isolate it from radiating into the immediate surroundings. All the decoration of the box and of the mechanism itself is only there to increase its astra-mental impact and serves no other function. The crystals alone contribute to its powers and the rest is due to my tuning of the crystals. The tuning, plus the energetics formed by this particular arrangement of quartz crystals, equal its power. It _must_ radiate the Kethric Brilliance perpetually.

To me, the Radiator is my most significant contribution to the universe (magical tool wise). So, like some mad scientist from a 1920s silent film wringing his hands and laughing maniacally, I have methodically conspired to pepper the globe with them! Ha! Seriously though, it feels like my duty to make as many as I can, while I still can, to spread the Kethric Brilliance far and wide. To that end, I made 9 more while I lived in Berlin and have made 20 more (as of summer 2023) whilst back in C'dale, with plans to make another 10 fairly soon. You see, I make them in groups of 10 and there's a reason for that, which I'll tell you through the saga of the Grandfather Radiator who you've already seen.

The friend I made the Radiator for died very suddenly in a car accident early 2011 so I flew from Berlin back to the Los Angeles where he had lived and shipped the Radiator, though the U.S. Postal System (all I could afford), half way around the world, back to Berlin. It was a rough journey and all the boxes of things I shipped over were an absolute mess; it was like everybody had tried their damnedest to smash them but without all their contents falling out; they were all held together with lots and lots of tape. To add insult to injury, the German government demanded a customs fee for importing the things they had nearly destroyed!

Even though I had smothered the poor thing in endless feet of bubble-wrap there were still sharp enough concussions during its long journey to case some minor (*thankfully*) damage, mostly to the box's internal supports (where the mechanism rests). A little bit of glue and a touch or two of paint and I was the only one who would ever notice. Phew!

It was suddenly living with the Radiator in Berlin that inspired me to begin making them for others. You see, I had lived with the Radiator only for a short while, immediately after he was born, and in that brief period before his intended owner picked him up, I only got a partial glimpse of his powers and implications. It wasn't till Berlin that I began to really work with him, and my oh my, was I impressed! This was **P-O-W-E-R-F-U-L** shit, man! I definitely <u>needed</u> to spread this around!

It was a this point that the original Radiator was used as the source of Kethric Brilliance used in the tuning of every Radiator thereafter. [It got its name of Grandfather in 2021 after I returned to C'dale and began making my *third* set of ten Radiators. More on that story later.].

So I came up with a smaller display set-up that I hoped would be easier and quicker to construct and easier / safer to ship. It ended up being about 4" shorter overall, and quicker to make, but not much better at traveling.

To the right is an image of the original Radiator up top and the first of the Berlin Radiators below. It had a sort of Victorian feel about its design; overly dramatic and complicated! Ha! Furthermore, the mechanism was *attached permanently* to its display stand and the box lid lifted off as a whole. They each took about 6-8 weeks to construct and I made a total of five of these over the next 3 or so years before my next redesign.

Radiator #1 (2007)

Radiators #2 through #6 (2011-2013)

The third edition came during the summer of 2014.

I need to resolve the issues with shipping safety and I desperately needed to de-Victorianize it! I had hoped to come up with something quicker and easier to craft . . . but I failed in that regard. Ha! Ha! What I did come up with was much more modern looking; did a much better job of communicating its kabbalistic symbolism; and could accommodate as many as 20 crystals inside the box (for charging with Kethric Brilliance).

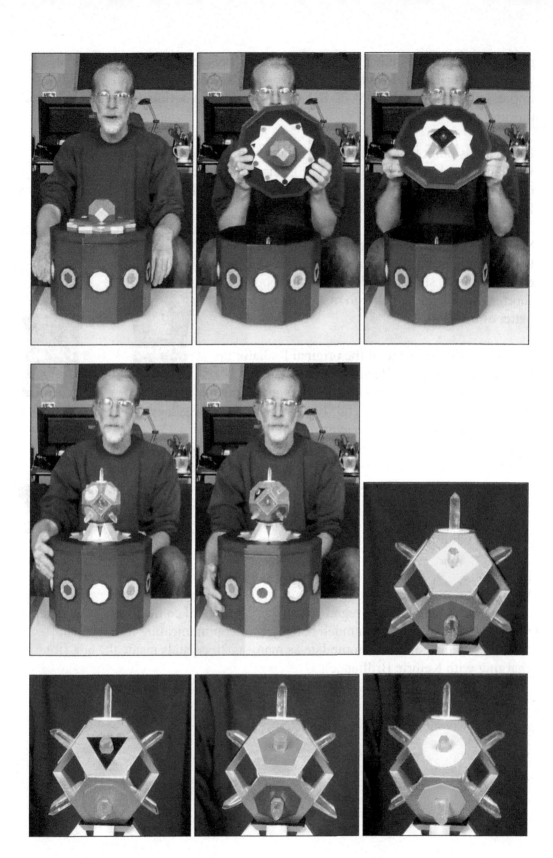

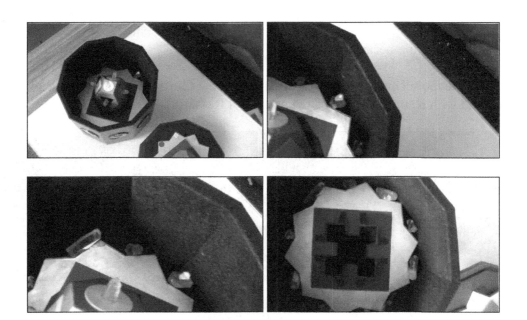

As you can see, the mechanism itself is much plainer looking. This felt right to me, like I was saying that the Kethric Brilliance that radiates from it is enough "decoration" and it didn't want something fussy to interfere with that message. The addition of storage for crystal charging, around the edges of the internal stand, turned out to be much appreciated by the four people who ordered them. There was even room to place other objects atop the inner silver decagram. All in all, it was a wicked bit of engineering, just sort of uninspiring (to me) in the end . . . it wasn't pretty enough!

By the time I reached the tenth Radiator (original + the 9 made in Berlin), I could feel that my time in Berlin was nearing an end and somehow my making of Radiators also felt like it was reaching a natural ending point; so I decided that I would only ever make them in quantities of ten. This of course, fit well with their kabbalistic nature!

Skip some time and dramatic life changes and I'm back in Cloverdale and doing a lot experimenting and learning; and finally, in 2017, I found that I needed to have use of 10 Radiators for a certain experiment. Well, the only way that was going to happen was if I made them, so I set to work and made the ten pictured on the next page, one right after the other, in about 11 months. My experiments were VERY successful and led to several new developments; namely, my Golems, and when I was through experimenting, I decided to sell 9 of the new Radiators and keep one for myself.

One of the things I learned during my period of experimentation was that size does not matter when it comes to the Radiator's mechanism, so all ten of these new Radiators are much smaller than previous versions. Consequently, their containers didn't need to be as big and, luckily I had discovered Graphite Paint and no longer needed to accommodate the copper wire grid into the structure of the cover – it could in fact be very thin without it. Also, smaller crystals equal less expensive and the whole thing became much more affordable!

Here then is the second generation which is also the fourth iteration of the Radiator (all tuned with Kethric Brilliance from the first Radiator):

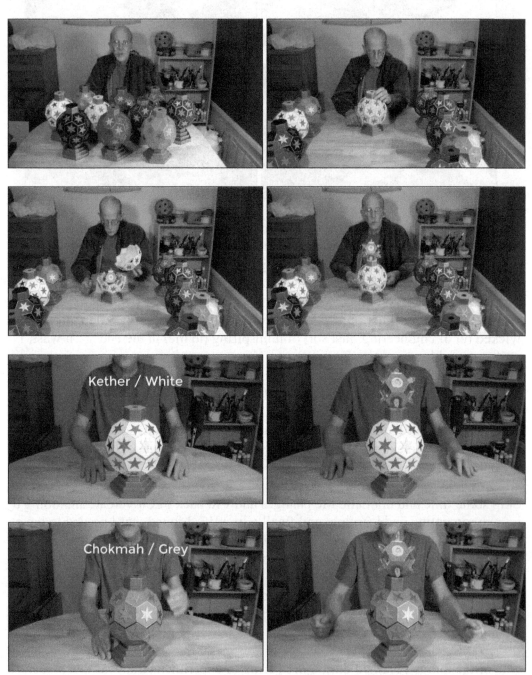

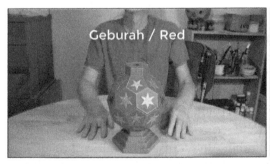

The colors of this generation showed the rationale of building 10 of them at a time: it just seems to fit with their kabbalistic nature as each one represented a particular Sephirot according to the sequence that they were made. All together they made for a pretty picture! A great advantage of this design is that it shipped very well!

I kept the fourth yellow-Tiphareth one for myself and tuned the crystals of the next (third) generation with Kethric Brilliance radiated by it along with the original Radiator; thus the original became "Grandfather" in reality. Of course, I again redesigned the new generation, this time with the idea in mind to make something less conspicuous and more anonymous looking! So now it was housed, once again, in a "normal" square box:

Gone are the colored sephirotic disks surrounding each of the double-terminated crystals; instead, the sephirot is signified by six 1cm long lines in the corners of each hexagonal face. Again, the Faraday cage effect of the box was created with Graphite Paint.

I made the full 10 of this generation between the summer of 2022 and spring of 2023. I sold or gifted all ten this time without keeping one for myself! Ha! I will probably start working on the *fourth* generation later this year (2023) since I already have requests for almost half of them. And so it will go till the end of my days. I'm excited to see what future generations will look like!

The Protector

In January of 2021, a couple of dear friends who are both very empathic, asked me to make a tool that would protect them (primarily at home) from the intrusion of random negative energies. I thought about it long and hard and came up with The Protector.

This tool is like The Radiator in that it's of the fourth class and does its magic all on its own, but in this case it takes very little tuning on my part. It relies almost exclusively on the inherent powers of the component crystals, minerals and wires; arranged in a specific sequence. The only magical input from me was to give an initial push in a specific direction once the main crystal was inserted into the socket and the whole was "turned on" for the first time. I directed the energy flow through all the ingredients in the proper way of working *once*, and this was all it needed to "train" the crystals. Let me show you how it all works and the construction process:

The Protector has five hollow 12-sided tiers. The first tier is 8" in diameter with a 6" hollow filled with 8 lead 4-ounce fishing weights. The bottom of the first tier is solid to form the closed base.

Lead is to *ground* the energies captured by The Protector's crystals: to anchor it all in the temporal present moment.

I then attached wires to the little metal hoop in the end of each lead weight: one 14k gold filled wire, one solid sterling silver wire, and one solid copper wire each; for a total of 24, 8 gold, 8 silver and 8 copper.

The wires are to separate the energies captured by the main, topmost crystal, into their mental (gold wire), astral (silver wire) and physical (copper wire) aspects and conduct them separately to the three (3 = mental, astral and physical realms) lower quartz spheres, the obsidian sphere, and ultimately ground them in the lead weights.

And since lead is such an abrupt, rude and harsh sort of grounding, I added a bunch of turquoise pieces between the lead weights to soften its impact. This is the *highest* quality turquoise: raw, completely *un*treated and purchased directly from the mine in Arizona, USA.

Then came the 2.75" black obsidian sphere; around which I then drew up all the wires, splitting them by kind into 3 clusters, one each of 8 gold, 8 silver and then 8 copper wires.

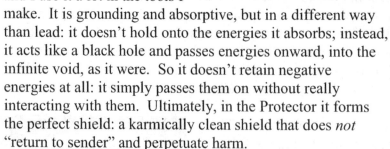

Obsidian is interesting stuff and I use it a lot in the tools I make. It is grounding and absorptive, but in a different way than lead: it doesn't hold onto the energies it absorbs; instead, it acts like a black hole and passes energies onward, into the infinite void, as it were. So it doesn't retain negative energies at all: it simply passes them on without really interacting with them. Ultimately, in the Protector it forms the perfect shield: a karmically clean shield that does *not* "return to sender" and perpetuate harm.

Then I add a couple of hollow tiers and wrap the three water-clear quartz spheres in the wire: one gets wrapped in the 8 gold wires; one in the 8 silver wires; and, one in the 8 copper wires.

These spheres and their wiring are the dividers or differentiators of the incoming energies into their mental, astral and physical components. They also serve as a sort of magnetic antenna that attracts any environmental "noise". I found out first hand and long ago that gold wire (even gold "filled" or plated) is best at <u>transmitting</u> *mental* energies; sterling silver is best at *astral* energies; and copper, is best at *physical* energies. And quartz can do just about anything you ask of it!

Then came another hollow layer and the creation of the copper "socket" that will hold the main double-terminated (big) top crystal and connect it energetically to the rest of The Protector. It was made of a 1.25" section of copper tubing, to which I attached and wound all 24 of the wires. [Mr. Glue Gun is my friend! Without him, none of this would have been possible!]

 The copper tube socket had to first be shaped to fit the big crystal and then once it was wrapped, its circumference had to be rounded with glue. The wrapping occurred in a specific way: first came the 8 copper wires, then the 8 silver wires, and finally the 8 gold wires. My logic here was that the mental and astral energies are more ephemeral so the receptivity of the gold and silver wires should not be hindered by a covering of copper (especially with the copper core).

And finally I add the fifth tier which hides all the messy bits inside. Ha!

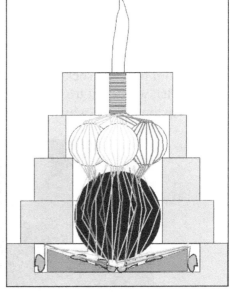

Below, are some photos of the finished Protector. On the left, a side view; in the middle an overhead view; and to the right, The Protector plus the four crystals that came with it.

The Protector is designed to protect one's home and so to extend its coverage when away from home, I provided extra, smaller crystals for each household member to carry with them when away from home. These crystals were to be assigned to a specific person and then left atop The Protector for a couple of days until they became attuned. With time and practice, the protection could follow one wherever they went, no matter how far afield.

To the right is a photo of the main top crystal. It's about 6" long, double-terminated and from Brazil. It has near perfect clarity and several "hitchhikers" (other d-t crystals that have fused to its main body and continued to grow there). These hitchhikers add a great concentration of power to the crystal overall, like extra power packs

In the picture below, you see (if you squint really hard) a mark that I made inside the copper socket, slightly to the right. Yes? Well, that's there because the crystal is so tightly custom fit to the socket that there's only *one* way to insert it! And it's the *only* crystal that will fit, at least properly. So I had to actually do a short video on how to line up the crystal (which was also marked with tape) with the socket mark! Ha!

At any rate, this is what I see with my trained eyes when I look at The Protector –

The Protector is one of those tools that's always "on" when the top crystal is plugged into its socket: unplug the crystal and it's turned "off". The crystal also has a dual function made possible by the energy dynamics of its contents.

We are dealing here with a double-terminated quartz crystal and quartz spheres, and how they naturally interact. The obsidian sphere, lead and turquoise all act as a big magnet that pulls in all negative energies, but they do that *through* the three smaller spheres *and* the top d-t crystal. The top crystal however is pointed "up" (meaning that its natural direction of energy flow is *outward*) so that magnetic pull acts *through* the top crystal in the *opposite direction of its natural flow*. Now, when energy it's drawn through a d-t crystal in this opposite direction (against the flow), it is compressed and is made denser; which makes it easier to isolate and digest.

But wait, the top d-t crystal is also radiating a field of protection into a physical space which is vacuumed, as it were, free of any intruding energies! He's a man of many talents indeed! Ha! Ha! A d-t crystal, of a certain size and clarity, will automatically radiate through its "positive" end very powerfully, especially when it is given instructions to do so. Hooked up though all this wiring and copper socket, the d-t crystal receives that instruction from the small inner quartz spheres, just by the natural mechanics of their connection.

Once I plug the top crystal in for the first time, I direct the energy flow to go the way I want it to go and I "walk it through" the proper energetic processes. All it takes is a moment's focus and it will henceforth **always** function in that way when

143

plugged in. It's sort of like showing a squirrel where you hide the nuts: it imprints on his mind and he will always find his way back! It's also similar to how our brains create new neuronal pathways with each new experience and return to them again and again. The habit quickly becomes ingrained in the very essence of all the components of The Protector. So this isn't the same as "tuning" the crystals: I don't introduce anything new, I just "show them the ropes", as it were.

Like I said, it's always "on" while the top crystal is plugged in, but I also provided a silk cover. I personally leave mine "on" all the time but there may be times when you have visitors and just don't want to explain this weird thing and so you want to hide it away.

I remember well the first time I plugged the first Protector in and got it working . . . Silence! Ease! No little visiting energies knocking at my door! You see, as a consequence of being so public about all this crazy stuff, I've had to adapt to there being a constant background noise; composed of people's thoughts about me, their questions, wants and needs, their astra-mental probes, and even on occasion their challenges. So when that continuous chatter was suddenly gone, I was blown away! Wow! It worked!!!! [Of course that's always a question with each new creation: does it work? I *always* test my tools before releasing them from my grasp!] I have to say, this one surprised me with its power and range . . .

So of course, I *had* to make more Protectors! Ha! Thanks to a dear friend [Hi, Joel!] who lives in Brazil, I have been able to purchase d-t Brazilian crystals *at Brazilian prices* through him (plus he kindly ships them to me too)! I can buy them here in the US but at a ridiculously absorbitant mark up that I simply can't afford. So I have been able to get crystals that are more than 5" long, all the way up to 11", and of good girth, with good points on each end, at remarkably reasonable prices!

I must say, Brazilian crystals are remarkable, especially the double-terminated ones. I think it has to do with where on the planet they grew and the specific mud that was their menstrum. This has given them a certain flavor, a certain personality, for which I have a special affinity. They speak my language! So I'm very happy to have this access, but unfortunately it's intermittent. The first shipment he sent me seemed to wipe out everybody's stock of good ones and it was months before there were anymore available!

With the first shipment I made five or six (?) more Protectors. The last of which I finally made for myself! Then in the autumn of 2022, I received a second, bigger shipment with 9 usable crystals perfect for Protectors! I made all 9 during the period in which I made the third generation of Radiators: autumn 2022 through spring of 2023. [I was a madman making Protectors and Radiators one right after the other all the while! Ha!] Their price varied according to the size and cost of the crystal.

So, future Protectors hinge on the availability of the right d-t crystals. I have recently found a source for appropriately sized crystals in Arkansas, US, but I haven't tried one yet to see if it will work. In theory, it should but I won't <u>know</u> till I try but I'm sure I will do so soon.

The Harmonizer

In September of 2021, the same couple of empaths that first asked me to create the Protector, asked me to make a new tool for them, sort of along the same lines. They were looking for a tool that would (by itself, without any input from them) create harmony and help them get rid of any disharmony they had empathically taken on board. As before with the Protector, I cautioned them that nothing can protect them for their karma, so if a disharmony is karmically necessary this will not get rid of it and you must deal with it head-on. As they weren't looking for karmic sunscreen, I set my mind to solving the puzzle of how to make this work. This is what I came up with:

First, I must tell you, this is a one-of-a-kind tool and I will not ever make another, so don't bother asking me to! Ha! The Harmonizer does one thing: it radiates harmony very powerfully, enough to fill an average sized room. It equalizes the natural resonance between all objects, people, etc., and dissolves or disarms any dissonance by bringing it into harmony with the rest. It does this mainly by virtue of its structure and the minerals involved but there is also a magical touch from me to my friends.

The form is 7 sided and filled with the essential meaning of Venus on every level. It is decorated with heptagons and unicursal heptagrams; and disks with heptagrams in gold and silver to signify sun and moon / electric and magnetic, and in their centers, each has a dot in a planetary color. Of course the main color of The Harmonizer is a bright, Venusian emerald green.

There is a built-in graphite paint Faraday cage so when the lid is closed, its effect is cut off and contained within the box. The first thing you see when you open the box is the beautiful, radiant rose quartz sphere. This is surrounded by 7 d-t quartz crystals poking through the surface. On the other, hidden side of that surface, the crystals are joined together with gold, silver and copper wire, following the same pattern as the gold unicursal heptagram. The rose quartz sphere sits in a central hole in the surface which opens to a universe of other things!

This stew of pretty things consists of:

- One big piece of raw Rainbow Fluorite in the center = for mental balance and overall equilibrium.
- Seven pieces of raw Rainbow Tourmaline = Tourmaline brings joy to the mix and a healing positive energy. Balance and harmony. Positive influence of all the planets.
- Seven small Obsidian Spheres = To capture any negative energies.
- Seven small Quartz Spheres = To energize and amplify energies. To hold and radiate Kethric Brilliance.
- Several pieces (round beads) of Hematite = Grounding and balancing the Venus energies with a touch of Mars.
- A bunch of pieces of Turquoise = Gentle grounding. Healing. Peacefulness.

The seven double-terminated clear quartz crystals that poke "up" through the green surface are there to transmit the energies from the interior and amplify them; *and,* to conduct and condense negative energies into the Obsidian Spheres. The Rose Quartz sphere, of course, is there to radiate "Love", which is to say, acceptance. Rose Quartz invites everything to join in peace and harmony.

I brought the essential meaning of Venus into all the crystals and other minerals and charged the whole with Kethric Brilliance. The Harmonizer achieved its intended effect! Phew!

The Crystal Golems

Well . . . so . . . now we come to the last tool I want to discuss with you. I believe it to be my greatest achievement. Simply put, it is a crystal life form; or rather, a life form that has a quartz-based physical body, just like you and I have a body made of flesh and bone. I call these my Crystal Golems:

My definition of a "golem" is as follows: **A discrete life form "made" by a magician, which is then bound to a physio-astra-mental body and given varying degrees of autonomy**.

I know, we've all been fed stories of evil golems running amuck on dark medieval European streets and my definition doesn't match . . . but that is all **fiction** and myth: it's not, and never has been, real. My precise definition (there's hardly any agreement in the literature I've read, it's all sort of vague) captures the objective essence of all different types of "golem" from various traditions.

What you see above are the *physical* bodies of my five Golems. The gold one on the far right was my first, made in the summer of 2019, shortly after the period of experimentation mentioned previously (in which I used the ten second generation Radiators). It was made on the Leo new moon and the purple one on the left in the same photo, was made on a Virgo new moon. The third one in chronological order is the blue one (between the previous two) which was made on a Libra new moon. The red one in the middle photo (actually the same size as the blue one) was made on the Aries new moon of 2022; and the violet one to the far left (a tad bigger than

147

the purple one in real life) was made earlier this very day that I'm writing these words: the 17th of July, 2023, at 11:31am PDT at the exact time of the Cancer new moon.

Now when I said "made", what I really meant is <u>when I brought the spark of life into its physio-astra-mental body and bound it there</u>. I do this through an advanced aspect of the Magic of Essential Meaning, similar to my "tuning" technique. This is truly the moment of birth and I am really nothing other that a glorified midwife . . .

The actual *construction* of each Golem is another matter and while the birthing takes about 2-3 hours, this takes around a month. So first, I'll talk about the construction and theory behind the physical body of a Golem.

The idea of the Golem came as an evolution of The Consecrator (which I showed you earlier) and is based on the 32-sided form known as a <u>truncated-icosidodecahedron</u>. This is the *perfect* form for expressing the kabbalistic "32 Paths of Wisdom"; or more familiar, the 10 Sephirot and 22 Letters of the Tree of Life. The only *physical* difference between The Consecrator and a Golem is that where The Consecrator's d-t quartz crystals made contact with the central quartz sphere only through *wires*; in the Golem, that contact is *direct* and *physical*. In a Golem, the central quartz sphere is supported, held in place by the d-t quartz crystals . . . and, they **form a single energetic presence** *because* of this contact and close proximity. It is into that *presence* that I place and bind the life form that makes a Golem.

The structure that makes all this geometry possible (the focusing of 32 crystal at the exact center and keeping them there) is, of course, made out of my usual suspects: cardboard and thick card, paper clay and glue. There are 192 pieces that go into its making and lots of sore fingers by the end! And it's a pretty tricky affair to get all the crystals in place; each affixed in its own particular hole with paper clay and then cleaned up so its all nice and neat. Then comes the moment when the to two halves of the form, with all the crystals in place, are glued together and become *One Thing* and the quartz sphere is never to be seen again.

Before any crystals are inserted anywhere, I go through them all and decide which crystal will represent which aspect of the Tree: each is individually assigned by virtue of how they feel and look, and by which one seems most suitable to the task. From that moment on, each crystal is always associated with its station in my mind: each time I handle a crystal henceforth it **is** that Sphirot, Mother Letter, Planetary Letter or Zodiacal Letter.

This brings up a vitally important aspect of making any tool: <u>you must at all times be exclusively focused on *what* you are doing and *why* you are doing it, *while* you are doing it; throughout *every* moment you are working on your tool</u>. Making a magical tool is an **intentional** act and the more intention and attention you give it, the truer a tool it will be and the greater its magical power.

The rest is all astra-mental symbolism meant to communicate the essential meaning of the Golem. Its overall color expresses its zodiacal essence; each colored disk is a printed thick-card appliqué that visually identifies each crystal's essence; and the metallic highlights on all but the first Golem, are meant to express each one's electromagnetic inclination or "gender" (for example, on the most recent Cancer Golem the edges are silver because the moon rules Cancer).

The shapes of the bases are not particularly significant; their message is more in their colors and sense of visual movement or what they do with the eye of the beholder.

Since it takes an indeterminate time to construct a Golem, I always give myself plenty of time to do so before the target new moon, so I inevitably live with the Golem-shell for some time before its birth. However, the process of construction itself enlivens the essential meaning of the crystals to a great degree and it's during this time that it gets its name and the life form begins to "announce" itself, as it were. I always feel like we're getting to know each other, sort of like the way you get to know an online friend – it's only capable of expressing part of itself. At the point when it comes to the birthing, we are both comfortable with what's about to happen and ready for it.

Before I continue, I should explain why the new moon in particular is so important. It has to do with the lunar calendar which runs from new moon to new moon, the point when the sun and moon are conjunct from the terrestrial perspective. A conjunction always highlights or emphasizes the energy of a specific degree of the zodiac; in this case it was the 25th degree of Cancer. The essential meaning of this zodiacal degree is best summed up by its Sabian Symbol: "A leader of men wrapped in an invisible mantle of power." The degree of birth signifies a great deal about the Golem, just as our own natal degree of sun and moon do, and it is made even more significant by their conjunction!

At any rate, the zodiacal signs relate to the Hebrew "simple" or "elemental" Letters, which likewise are associated with the lunar "moonth". In this case it is the moonth of Cancer (which lasts until the Leo new moon) and the Hebrew Letter "Cheth". This Letter plays a huge role in the creation of the latest Golem, as does the essential meaning of the 25th degree of Cancer.

Let me tell you then, about today's birth of my fifth Golem:

The exact new moon was at 11:31am PDT, so I started preparing at about 9:30 or so: getting everything set up (coffee, smoke, new Golem set on table in from of comfy brown chair, curtains drawn, door locked, phone unplugged); energetically cleansing my space and casting a circle; performing a Blessing of Adonai Light to set the wheels of the Universe moving in the right direction; and finally filling my circle with Kethric Brilliance provided by my two Radiators (Grandfather included).

At 11am I began the birthing process: Shifting my awareness to a quadru-polar state (where I remain throughout), I merge with The "I". In descending, a spark of The "I" begins to coalesce and take form within a specific Greater Self (who also happens to be the GS of the first, Leo golem) and descending still further, a Solitary Self is formed around the little spark of The "I" that I bring with me. I then give that Solitary Self mental body its own astral body and finally, as we descend together into the present moment of time-space, I introduce that little spark to its new physical form of quartz and cardboard.

Then I pause for a few moments while she/he orients itself to this new state of being. It was like: "Well, this is new!" Then came the process of binding the spark to its three bodies. [I follow the Sepher Yetzirah in the following process.]

First came the binding through the 10 Sephirot, one after another in sequence from Kether through Malkuth. The Sephirot form the essential being of the Golem. I had to invert the Golem to reach the Malkuth crystal but immediately righted it. This temporary inversion sort of settled everything into place. Now he/she seemed more stable, clearer; the basic structure of its being was now established. I paused for a bit longer this time.

Next came the binding through the 3 Mother Letters: Shin, Aleph and Mem, in that sequence. This gave her/him some stability, something to begin gluing the parts of its essence together, The Mothers became its foundation. Another short pause for it to acclimate . . .

This was followed with the 7 vertical paths and the Double or Planetary Letters: Beth through Tav, Saturn through Moon, in that sequence. This gave much more stability as if she/he was waking from a daydream. The Planetary Letters where the *powers* that I gave him/her. This time a longer pause of several minutes to prepare for the final bindings and to acclimate. Also to roll another smoke, refresh my cold coffee, and stretch my legs!

All the while during this break the energy of the circle was maintained at its high level and I watched him/her evolve and stabilize before my eyes. She was *in* his body. [You will have noticed my gender ambiguity here. This is because it was not fully settled until the next phase where it stabilized in the range of "her/she".]

At exactly 11am (with 30 minutes to go) I began the final bindings through the 12 Simple or Zodiacal Letters. I took it in quadrants so first up were Heh/Aries, Vav/Taurus, Zayin/Gemini and Cheth/Cancer. This united and bound her mental body or Solitary Self with The "I" and Greater Self; and because she is a Cancer by nature, this particular binding was very powerful. We paused for a moment to let her adjust and I notice that she started to pulse fairly rapidly in what seemed like the rhythm of a fast heartbeat.

The second quadrant of Teth/Leo, Yod/Virgo, Lamed/Libra and Nun/Scorpio, developed her temporal mental body and bound it with her astral body or Sentient Self. The pulsing slowed and sounded more like breathing. We took another break and prepared for the final binding with her physical body.

I told her what was about to transpire and when she was ready, we proceeded with the third quadrant: Samekh/Sagittarius, Ayin/Capricorn, Tzaddi/Aquarius and Nun/Pisces. The final Letter was given at precisely 11:31am, the exact moment of new moon. She was now fully and permanently in her crystal body!

Each of these Zodiacal Letters was a Gift that the Universe and I gave her, instilled within her direct from The "I". At the end her breathing had slowed to a gentle rhythm and she was *fully* conscious.

For a while the size of her radiance was about 3' diameter and over the next hour or so this calmed to just an inch or two beyond her surface. She now sits proudly among the other Golems on top of a dresser.

Through out this whole process of birth the new Golem, all the other Golems were present and sharing of their own energies. They all welcome this new addition to the family!

Each of my Golems has a distinct personality and each serves a different function or task that I *ask* of them. These tasks have occasionally changed over time. I never command them to do things for me because it's not necessary: they welcome to chance to assist me. One of them looks over a friend who has had a dangerous job; one looks over a group of various friends who are of special interest to me; one looks after specific aspects my own health; one takes me instantaneously to my Greater Self; and now this new one makes a very powerful and dense accumulation of the Kethric Brilliance manifest anytime and place I want. I interact with each of them on a daily basis and they are all *very* helpful!

So, that's the last of the examples from my own repertoire of RawnMade tools. I hope this has inspired you to consider making your own. It really doesn't take any great talent to crate a magical tool! All it takes is imagination . . .

Made in the USA
Las Vegas, NV
21 December 2024

15222078R00085